Genetic Engineering

OPPOSING VIEWPOINTS®

Genetic
engineering

Genetic Engineering

OPPOSING VIEWPOINTS®

Other Books of Related Interest

Genetic Engineering
OPPOSING VIEWPOINTS®

James D. Torr, *Book Editor*

David L. Bender, *Publisher*
Bruno Leone, *Executive Editor*
Bonnie Szumski, *Editorial Director*
Stuart Miller, *Managing Editor*

OPPOSING
VIEWPOINTS®
SERIES

Greenhaven Press, Inc., San Diego, California

Cover photo: John Foxx Images; Metaphotos;
© Pioneer Hi-Bred International, Inc.

Library of Congress Cataloging-in-Publication Data

Genetic engineering / James D. Torr, book editor.
    p.   cm. — (Opposing viewpoints)
    Includes bibliographical references and index.
    ISBN 0-7377-0511-6 (pbk. : alk. paper) —
ISBN 0-7377-0512-4 (lib. bdg. : alk. paper)
    1. Genetic engineering. 2. Genetic engineering—Social
aspects. 3. Genetic engineering—Moral and ethical aspects.
I. Torr, James D., 1974– . II. Series.

QH442.G4432 2001
660.6'5—dc21

00-28335
CIP

Greenhaven Press, Inc., P.O. Box 289009
San Diego, CA 92198-9009

> "Congress shall make
> no law...abridging the
> freedom of speech, or of
> the press."

First Amendment to the U.S. Constitution

The basic foundation of our democracy is the First
Amendment guarantee of freedom of expression. The
Opposing Viewpoints Series is dedicated to the
concept of this basic freedom and the idea that it is
more important to practice it than to enshrine it.

Contents

Why Consider Opposing Viewpoints?

"The only way in which a human being can make some approach to knowing the whole of a subject is by hearing what can be said about it by persons of every variety of opinion and studying all modes in which it can be looked at by every character of mind. No wise man ever acquired his wisdom in any mode but this."

John Stuart Mill

In our media-intensive culture it is not difficult to find differing opinions. Thousands of newspapers and magazines and dozens of radio and television talk shows resound with differing points of view. The difficulty lies in deciding which opinion to agree with and which "experts" seem the most credible. The more inundated we become with differing opinions and claims, the more essential it is to hone critical reading and thinking skills to evaluate these ideas. Opposing Viewpoints books address this problem directly by presenting stimulating debates that can be used to enhance and teach these skills. The varied opinions contained in each book examine many different aspects of a single issue. While examining these conveniently edited opposing views, readers can develop critical thinking skills such as the ability to compare and contrast authors' credibility, facts, argumentation styles, use of persuasive techniques, and other stylistic tools. In short, the Opposing Viewpoints Series is an ideal way to attain the higher-level thinking and reading skills so essential in a culture of diverse and contradictory opinions.

In addition to providing a tool for critical thinking, Opposing Viewpoints books challenge readers to question their own strongly held opinions and assumptions. Most people form their opinions on the basis of upbringing, peer pressure, and personal, cultural, or professional bias. By reading carefully balanced opposing views, readers must directly confront new ideas as well as the opinions of those with whom they disagree. This is not to simplistically argue that everyone who reads opposing views will—or should—change his or her opinion. Instead, the series enhances readers' understanding of their own views by encouraging confrontation with opposing ideas. Careful examination of others' views can lead to the readers' understanding of the logical inconsistencies in their own opinions, perspective on why they hold an opinion, and the consideration of the possibility that their opinion requires further evaluation.

Evaluating Other Opinions

To ensure that this type of examination occurs, Opposing Viewpoints books present all types of opinions. Prominent spokespeople on different sides of each issue as well as well-known professionals from many disciplines challenge the reader. An additional goal of the series is to provide a forum for other, less known, or even unpopular viewpoints. The opinion of an ordinary person who has had to make the decision to cut off life support from a terminally ill relative, for example, may be just as valuable and provide just as much insight as a medical ethicist's professional opinion. The editors have two additional purposes in including these less known views. One, the editors encourage readers to respect others' opinions—even when not enhanced by professional credibility. It is only by reading or listening to and objectively evaluating others' ideas that one can determine whether they are worthy of consideration. Two, the inclusion of such viewpoints encourages the important critical thinking skill of objectively evaluating an author's credentials and bias. This evaluation will illuminate an author's reasons for taking a particular stance on an issue and will aid in readers' evaluation of the author's ideas.

As series editors of the Opposing Viewpoints Series, it is our hope that these books will give readers a deeper understanding of the issues debated and an appreciation of the complexity of even seemingly simple issues when good and honest people disagree. This awareness is particularly important in a democratic society such as ours in which people enter into public debate to determine the common good.

Those with whom one disagrees should not be regarded as enemies but rather as people whose views deserve careful examination and may shed light on one's own.

Thomas Jefferson once said that "difference of opinion leads to inquiry, and inquiry to truth." Jefferson, a broadly educated man, argued that "if a nation expects to be ignorant and free . . . it expects what never was and never will be." As individuals and as a nation, it is imperative that we consider the opinions of others and examine them with skill and discernment. The Opposing Viewpoints Series is intended to help readers achieve this goal.

David L. Bender & Bruno Leone,
Series Editors

Greenhaven Press anthologies primarily consist of previously published material taken from a variety of sources, including periodicals, books, scholarly journals, newspapers, government documents, and position papers from private and public organizations. These original sources are often edited for length and to ensure their accessibility for a young adult audience. The anthology editors also change the original titles of these works in order to clearly present the main thesis of each viewpoint and to explicitly indicate the opinion presented in the viewpoint. These alterations are made in consideration of both the reading and comprehension levels of a young adult audience. Every effort is made to ensure that Greenhaven Press accurately reflects the original intent of the authors included in this anthology.

Introduction

"Genetic engineering poses moral and social dilemmas every bit as daunting as the rewards are enticing."
—*bioethicist Stephen P. Stich*

Genetic engineering is the process of taking DNA from one organism and inserting it into another. The first instances of genetic engineering in the 1970s involved bacteria whose DNA could spontaneously recombine with other strains of bacteria—hence genetic engineering is often referred to as "recombinant DNA technology." Since these first experiments in gene swapping between microorganisms, scientists have become more adept at splicing genes between organisms and even between species. Terms such as "gene transfer," "gene therapy," and "bioengineering" have been coined as these processes have become more sophisticated and precise.

Cloning is a new technology that is very closely related to genetic engineering. The cloning of a sheep in 1997 by researcher Ian Wilmut involved many breakthroughs in the biological manipulation of mammalian cells—however, the genetic makeup of the resulting sheep, Dolly, was not altered. "Biotechnology" is the broader term that is often used to encompass cloning and other technologies that may rely only partially on genetic engineering.

The use of bovine growth hormone by dairy farmers is another example of how the line between biotechnology and genetic engineering may be blurred. In the 1980s scientists isolated the gene that produces bovine somatotropin, a naturally occurring hormone that causes cows to produce more milk. They used genetic engineering to create bacteria that would produce recombinant bovine somatotropin (rBST). Many farmers now inject their cows with rBST, and this practice has become part of the debate over genetically engineered food. However, neither the cows nor their milk has been genetically engineered.

Because the scope of genetic engineering is so vast—the ability to manipulate DNA, after all, can potentially be used on any living thing—it is not surprising that biotechnology has such a wide variety of possible applications. One avenue that has already been widely explored is the genetic engineering of bacteria to produce vaccines, hormones, or any other biological product. Bovine growth hormone is one controversial application of this technology, but on the other hand, the use of bacteria to mass-produce human insulin for diabetics has met with almost unanimous praise.

The genetic engineering of plants and animals is also underway. Genetic engineering of higher organisms has progressed less rapidly, however, both because of the ethical concerns involved and because plant and animal genomes are far more complex than those of bacteria. Nonetheless, genetically modified food crops are a reality. Roughly a third of the corn grown in the United States contains the genes of the bacteria *Baccilus thuringiensis*, which produces a substance that kills certain insects. While the genetic manipulation of plants, in the form of cross-breeding different strains to produce more vigorous hybrids, has been occurring for millennia, the insertion of specific genes from other species into plant genomes could not be done without modern tools of genetic engineering.

For the most part, however, these applications of genetic engineering have met with relatively little fanfare; it is the prospect of genetically engineering humans that has aroused the most public interest. Gene therapy—the use of biotechnology to treat genetic diseases—has been the most anticipated use of genetic engineering in humans. W. French Anderson, one of the pioneers in this area of research, hails genetic engineering as a "fourth revolution in medicine" that will transform medicine just as improved sanitation, the discovery of anesthesia, and the development of vaccines and antibiotics did.

However, the prospect of altering the human genome has raised concerns that the technology could be abused. "Eugenics" is the term most often associated with the abuse of genetic research. First coined by Sir Francis Galton in 1883, the term has come to describe proposals in the 1920s to "breed better human beings" and eliminate the "genetically unfit." These early theories about what constituted a "good" gene were often racist, and the eugenics movement fell into disgrace when the Nazis used its theories to justify the elimination of people they deemed genetically inferior. Given the dark history of eugenics, it is not surprising that modern proposals to "improve" humans through genetic engineering are often met with suspicion.

Yet in the face of so much opposition to genetic engineering—protests against bioengineered food, predictions that the technology will be abused, and so on—there has been a backlash of sorts among biotech enthusiasts. For example, *Reason* magazine science correspondent Ronald Bailey writes that biotechnology "could one day be used to grow new heart, nerve, pancreatic, or liver cells that would replace tissues damaged by disease," but he warns that these treatments "are just the sort of ambitious, 'unnatural' technologies the luddicons fear."

In comparing anti-biotechnology activists to Luddites, the nineteenth-century English craftsmen who destroyed the textile machinery that was displacing them, Bailey is suggesting that people who oppose genetic engineering oppose science and progress in general. Or, as he puts it, "the battle over the future of biotech, . . . is between those who fear what humans, having eaten of the Tree of Knowledge of Good and Evil, might do with biotech and those who think that it is high time that we also eat of the Tree of Life."

In many people's view, genetic engineering offers the ability to literally alter life itself; the questions surrounding biotechnology reflect a larger debate about whether society should place limits on scientific and technological progress. The authors in *Genetic Engineering: Opposing Viewpoints* explore these issues in the following chapters: How Will Genetic Engineering Affect Society? Is the Genetic Engineering of Humans Ethical? How Does Genetic Engineering Affect Food and Agriculture? How Should Genetic Engineering Be Regulated? Throughout this anthology, authors present conflicting views about genetic engineering and its consequences for mankind.

CHAPTER 1

How Will Genetic Engineering Affect Society?

Chapter Preface

Proponents of genetic engineering claim that the technology promises enormous benefits for medicine, agriculture, and industry. Yet, like nuclear power, biotechnology has aroused considerable public concern because it is perceived by many as an unpredictable—and hence dangerous—technology.

Science critic Jeremy Rifkin warns that "whenever a genetically engineered organism is released, there is always a small chance that it . . . will run amok because, like nonindigenous species, it has been artificially introduced into a complex environment. . . . While there is only a small chance of it triggering an environmental explosion, if it does, the consequences could be significant and irreversible." Bioethicist Leon Kass warns that the genetic engineering of humans is very different from other medical treatments: "Medicine treats only existing individuals, and it treats them only remedially, seeking to correct deviations from a more or less stable norm of health. Genetic engineering, by contrast, will . . . deliberately make changes that are transmissible into succeeding generations."

Defenders of genetic engineering do not deny that the technology is without risks, but they argue that the dangers associated with genetic engineering are exaggerated. Henry Miller, a former director of the Office of Biotechnology at the Food and Drug Administration, believes that activists opposed to genetic engineering suffer from technophobia—the fear of new technology. "In earlier era," he writes, "techno-skeptics predicted electrocution from the first telephones, believed Jenner's early attempts at smallpox vaccination would create monsters, and doubted the possibility of matching blood for transfusions. Today, they warn of Andromeda Strains and Jurassic Parks resulting from recombinant DNA–modified organisms."

Many observers feel that the controversies surrounding genetic engineering are part of a larger debate over whether scientific progress ultimately benefits or harms society. The viewpoints in the following chapter examine the potential benefits and dangers of genetic engineering in greater detail.

> *"[Genetic engineering] holds great potential to bolster the health, food resources, and economies of all people."*

Genetic Engineering Will Benefit Society

David A. Christopher

In the following viewpoint, David A. Christopher describes various ways in which genetic engineering techniques could be used to improve medicine, industry, agriculture, and the environment. He maintains that genetic engineering will someday be used to cure genetic diseases, produce inexpensive medicines, and breed superior plants and animals. He also predicts that scientists will genetically engineer bacteria to produce fuel and degrade toxic chemicals and other pollutants into harmless compounds such as carbon dioxide. Christopher is associate professor in the Department of Plant Molecular Physiology and Molecular Biosciences and Biosystems Engineering at the University of Hawaii.

As you read, consider the following questions:

1. How does the author define the term "recombinant DNA technology"?
2. What term does Christopher use to describe the practice of using farm animals as factories for medicines and pharmaceuticals?
3. How does the author define the term "bioremediation"?

The desire to improve our world is inherently human. From our homes and cars to our health and food, we regularly strive to enhance what we have. With the biotechnology age upon us, this desire is being channeled in directions that were previously unforeseen. In the past 50 years, we have learned a great deal about genes—their structure, function, and how to manipulate them. It has thus become feasible to engineer genes, to impart new traits into living things and their underlying biological processes. Scientists are therefore applying the methods of genetic engineering to provide society with novel tools to improve agriculture, medicine, industry, and the environment.

Efforts to genetically modify living things are not, however, unique to modern society, for they go back thousands of years. Early people had an innate understanding of genetic principles when they learned to cross-breed the most vigorous plants from their fields. For instance, every corn plant grown in the United States today is the result of genetic modifications introduced not only by today's scientists but also by Native Americans, who selected strains of maize for improved characteristics over the past 7,000 years or more.

Nowadays, geneticists harness the natural genetic recombination processes that occur in cells to directly alter and transfer pieces of DNA from one organism to another and from a test tube to recipient cells. The manipulation of pieces of DNA to produce new DNA combinations is referred to as recombinant DNA technology, which forms the basis of genetic engineering. This technology is being applied to an amazingly diverse range of problems, from curing human disease and making caffeine-free coffee beans to cleaning up oil spills and recycling waste. The list of applications grows daily.

The Promise of Gene Therapy

Many diseases, including a number of cancers, are caused by defective genes. Drug treatments for such diseases generally remedy just the symptoms and frequently cause side effects. In addition, treatments that replace missing enzymes require repeated injections, and organ transplants may be rejected by the body's immune system. Given that there are more than 4,000 genetic diseases, and cancers lead to over 500,000 deaths in the United States each year, it is clear that new treatments are necessary. One promising approach is gene therapy—a type of treatment in which the doctor introduces a beneficial gene into a patient's cells to produce a vital protein that the patient lacks or to inhibit the activity of disease-causing genes. Gene therapy has the potential to correct the root cause of the disorder, and the patient's immune system does not reject his own genetically altered cells.

How can good genes be inserted into sick cells? One way is to place them in viruses, which are adept at injecting their genes into the cells they infect. But because viruses themselves can cause diseases, scientists first disarm them by removing the harmful genes, then add the "good" gene to the virus. While the virus is robbed of its capacity to reproduce, it is able to transfer the beneficial gene to the appropriate cells.

The first human gene-therapy trial was started in September 1990 by a research team—including Drs. W. French Anderson, R. Michael Blaese, and Kenneth Culver—at the National Institutes of Health. The patient was a four-year-old girl who suffered from severe combined immunodeficiency disease (SCID), which seriously impaired her immune system and made her extremely vulnerable to infections. In her case, the disease was caused by a single defective gene for the enzyme known as adenosine deaminase (ADA). This defect causes toxic levels of adenosine and deoxyadenosine to accumulate in the blood, killing the germ-fighting B and T cells (lymphocytes).

Using a disarmed virus as a gene shuttle, the normal ADA gene was introduced into a batch of T cells previously removed from the child. About every three months for the next two years, she received transfusions with her own genetically engineered T cells, which began synthesizing normal ADA. In that time period, she became increasingly able to resist infection and began to lead a more normal life.

Given the success of the above trial, this type of therapy was expanded to include more patients. But one problem with using T cells for genetic engineering is that they eventually die. Scientists are now focusing on genetically modifying bone-marrow stem cells, which lead to the production of all blood cells, including immune cells. In principle, stem cells could serve as a continuous source of healthy blood cells for a lifetime. . . .

Further development of gene therapy will involve producing gene-delivery systems that are more efficient and have higher capacity, but the construction of such systems is a major hurdle that remains to be crossed. Also, in the future, tissue-specific viruses that infect just one type of tissue (such as tumor, lung, or brain) will be used. For example, a tumor-seeking herpes virus is being used to introduce a gene for an enzyme that converts the drug ganciclovir to a toxin that kills the tumor. As we expand human trials, develop better gene-delivery systems, and identify disease-causing genes, doctors will be prescribing gene therapy more frequently for many diseases.

Before attempting clinical trials on humans, researchers perform genetic-engineering experiments on animals, particularly mice, which are valuable model systems for human ailments, including Alzheimer's, arthritis, cancer, muscular dystrophy, high blood pressure, heart disease, and even hair loss. For instance, scientists have reproduced Alzheimer's disease in mice by modifying genes believed to be responsible for the disorder. By so doing, they can use the mice to assess treatments and conduct studies that would be virtually impossible to do on human subjects. Although information obtained from studies on mice cannot always be applied to people, many key insights into human diseases and their treatments are being gained.

Medicines in Milk and Vaccines in Vegetables

Recently, genetically engineered mice were designed to secrete medicines in their milk. For example, a reliable supply of the scarce protein cystic fibrosis transmembrane regulator (CFTR) is needed for strategies to cure cystic fibrosis. The gene for CFTR was engineered with signals to allow CFTR to be expressed in mammary cells and deposited in the milk of lactating mice. It is anticipated that the mammary glands of farm animals will someday be used as factories for producing larger quantities of medicines and pharmaceuticals in milk—a process known as "pharming." Advantages of this method are that milk is easy to harvest and the medicine may be administered simply by drinking the milk. Alternatively, purifying the protein is efficient because milk contains only a small number of other proteins.

Scientists are also learning how to redesign genes for antibodies and vaccines to combat disease. Antibodies are proteins made by the body's immune system to fight infection by binding to germs and foreign substances in the blood. Vaccines stimulate antibody production. In one treatment for infection by HIV (the virus that is believed to cause AIDS), a gene for the drug exotoxin A is linked to a gene for the antibody, resulting in the production of a hybrid protein. The antibody seeks out and binds to the infected cells, and the attached drug kills them.

Intriguingly, some researchers are developing edible vaccines to fight hepatitis B and bacterial diarrhea by genetically altering plants, such as potato and banana. The transformed plants produce proteins that elicit immune responses in people who eat them.

Bacteria as Factories

Before recombinant DNA technology was developed, the high costs and limited quantities of most protein drugs restrained their development and use for treating disease. Now, harmless strains of bacteria have been genetically engineered with human genes to produce plentiful quantities of various protein medicines, such as insulin (to control diabetes), hemoglobin (to prevent anemia), and nerve growth factor (to repair nerves). The worldwide market for these types of drugs is estimated to be worth around $17–18 billion. Future research is focused on increasing production using new bacterial strains and special DNA pieces (called promoters) that enhance gene expression. Also, portions of proteins that cause side effects are being removed, leaving only the therapeutic segments.

Each year, the worldwide production of antibiotics amounts to roughly 100,000 tons, valued at about $5 billion. To obtain higher yields at lower production costs, certain species of soil bacteria (genus Streptomyces) have been genetically modified to increase the expression of antibiotic-producing genes. Furthermore, the structures of some antibiotics are being altered by genetic manipulations to develop new versions that kill antibiotic-resistant bacteria.

In addition, the production of a variety of commercially important enzymes can be enhanced by inserting new and

The Many Medical Applications of Biotechnology

The biomedical revolution of the next century promises to alter our culture, our politics, and our lives. It promises to extend our life span and to enhance our mental and physical capacities. . . .

On the horizon are artificial chromosomes containing genes that protect against HIV, diabetes, prostate and breast cancer, and Parkinson's disease, all of which could be introduced into a developing human embryo. When born, the child would have a souped-up immune system. Even more remarkably, artificial chromosomes could be designed with "hooks" or "docking stations," so that new genetic upgrades later could be slotted into the chromosomes and expressed in adults. Artificial chromosomes could also be arranged to replicate only in somatic cells, which form regular tissues, and not in the germ cells involved in reproduction. As a result, genetically enhanced parents would not pass those enhancements on to their children; they could choose new or different enhancements for their children, or have them born without any new genetic technologies. . . .

Meanwhile, the prospect of substantially extending the human lifespan is growing, as biomedical researchers investigate promising technologies to diagnose and treat the various ways the body breaks down with age. EntreMed Inc. of Rockville, Maryland, and Cell Genesys Inc. of Foster City, California, are working to deliver a gene-based drug that will cut off a cancer's blood supply and kill it. Human Genome Sciences, also of Rockville, is developing a heart-bypass-in-a-shot using the VEGF-2 gene, which produces a protein that encourages the growth of blood vessels around blocked arteries. In Silicon Valley, Santa Clara–based Affymetrix Inc. has created a "biochip"—a silicon wafer that analyzes thousands of genes in a single test, diagnosing all sorts of diseases. Combined with the full sequence of all human genes, which will be available in a couple of years, the biochip will enable doctors to do a full genetic physical with a simple blood test.

Ronald Bailey, *Reason*, December 1999.

modified genes (that encode the enzymes) into the cells of bacteria, yeast, insects, and plants. The enzymes may be the desired end products or they may be needed to produce other important substances. Examples of industrially produced enzymes include alpha-amylase (for alcohol production), bromelain and papain (to tenderize meat), and rennet (for cheese making). By extension, this approach can be used to give enzymes new properties, such as superior activity, enhanced specificity, and greater stability at higher temperatures—properties crucial to efficiency in the industrial setting. Similar techniques are being used to make dyes, such as indigo; amino acids, useful as nutrition boosters; and biopolymers, including adhesives, elastics, biodegradable plastics, rubber, and gums.

Genetic engineering is playing an important role in the recycling of starch and fiber wastes produced by the food and agriculture industries. Researchers are equipping microbes with genes to convert starch (present in potatoes and grain) and cellulose and lignin (present in wood, paper, and farm refuse) into simple sugars. And genes for enzymes involved in fermentation have been modified and placed in various bacteria and yeasts for faster conversion of simple sugars into ethanol. The ethanol can then be used as fuel. This approach is cleaner and more energy-efficient than industrial processes that require strong acids or bases and create toxic wastes.

On the Farm

Genetic engineering is being applied to all aspects of agriculture. For instance, dairy cattle can be genetically modified to increase the content of the milk protein casein. Casein levels directly affect the amount of cheese produced. Also high on the list is to make cows, sheep, goats, and pigs leaner and more resistant to diseases, to reduce the costs of vaccination, hormones, and drugs. But the genetic engineering of farm animals is inefficient and needs improvement.

Plant genetic engineering has progressed faster than that of mammals, because efficient delivery systems have been developed for inserting genes in plants, and it is relatively easy to regenerate an entire plant from a single genetically altered cell. In 1998, the United States had about 55 million acres of genetically engineered corn, soybean, and cotton, as estimated by the U.S. Department of Agriculture. The goal of crop genetic engineering is to reduce farm production costs and pesticide use and to increase yield and nutritional content.

The first genetically engineered and commercialized insect-resistant crop was the NewLeaf Russet Burbank potato, which is highly resistant to the Colorado potato beetle. It was created using the gene for Bt toxin, a natural insecticidal protein made by the bacterium Bacillus thuringiensis. Bt genes from different strains of the microbe have been engineered into corn, cotton, tomato, potato, tobacco, rice, apple, eggplant, cabbage, canola, alfalfa, walnut, poplar, spruce, and cranberry. Insect attack is markedly reduced, circumventing the need to spray with expensive and hazardous insecticides. The toxin destroys the digestive system of certain insects, such as caterpillars and rootworms, but it does not persist in the environment and is safe for people, other mammals, and fish. Future research is focused on creating more potent versions of Bt, to expand the types of insects controlled and to reduce the development of insect resistance to Bt.

To protect crops from serious viral damage, a method known as "cross-protection" has been applied. It involves inserting a viral gene into the plant's cells, so that the plant begins to express a piece (usually the outer coat protein) of the virus. Such transgenic plants resist infection entirely or display greatly reduced symptoms, as if they were naturally vaccinated against the virus. Scientists do not understand how cross-protection works, but they have used it to make numerous crops resistant to various viruses. The impact of this technology cannot be underestimated. For example, creation of a genetically engineered papaya that resists ringspot virus infection saved a nearly devastated industry in Hawaii.

Many crops are now being engineered to survive spraying with biodegradable herbicides. These herbicide-resistant plants were created by altering their protein targets that bind the herbicide and by adding genes for enzymes that destroy the herbicide. This approach encourages the use of biodegradable herbicides, such as glyphosate.

Genetic engineers are learning to design canola, soybean, and palm to produce everything from improved oils to plastics. Oils rich in oleic acid are preferred for cooking, while stearic acid is a raw material for soaps and detergents, and ricinoleic acid is valuable for industrial lubricants. A number of researchers have engineered plants with genes to make natural, biodegradable plastics that can lower our dependence on petroleum products and reduce garbage levels in landfills.

Some scientists are developing caffeine-free coffee beans by genetically inhibiting the gene that controls caffeine synthesis. Others are working to raise the levels of nutrients, such as vitamin E, carotenoids, flavonoids, and glucosinolates, which are naturally present in avocado, carrots, tea, and broccoli, respectively. And the protein content of corn is being enhanced. Clinical research suggests that elevated intake of vitamins and phytochemicals reduces the risk of developing cancers and cardiovascular disease and slows some aging processes. The low micronutrient levels in staple crops such as wheat, rice, potatoes, and cassava lead to deficient diets for 800 million people worldwide. Thus, using genetic engineering to increase the nutritional value of food is an especially exciting development with enormous potential benefits.

In the future, plant genetic engineers will be tackling almost every trait imaginable. Efforts are under way to create crops that are more tolerant of drought, saltwater, heat, ultraviolet radiation, and injury by freezing. Even aging, sweetness, flower color, and fragrance are being altered by plant geneticists. These scientists will soon be focusing more on putting multiple genes for many traits—such as resistance to insects, fungi, viruses, bacteria, and herbicides—into one plant variety.

Microbes with an Appetite for Poison

Genetic engineering is proving to be invaluable for bioremediation—the use of living systems to convert pollutants and poisonous wastes to nontoxic substances. Ever since the use of oil-eating bacteria to clean up the oil spill from the tanker Exxon Valdez in Alaska in 1984, scientists have greatly expanded the repertoire of microbial bioremediation. They have been using genes for enzymes that enable bacteria to consume and degrade hazardous chemicals (including phenols, trichloroethylene, and pesticides) and suspected carcinogens (such as methylene chloride, polychlorinated biphenyls, and toluene). The microbes degrade the compounds into carbon dioxide and other harmless products. Such microbes can be applied to contaminated sites or housed in "bioreactors" used in treating industrial wastes.

These efforts demonstrate the feasibility of engineering microbes to degrade a variety of chemicals. But one limitation is that microbes respond unpredictably to changes in the soil, temperature, moisture, and nutrients. Future research is geared toward engineering bacteria to expand the range of chemicals they can degrade in various environments. For example, researchers have created microbes that tolerate colder temperatures while consuming toxins. Such microbes can be monitored in the field by tagging them with the lux genes for bioluminescence—the types of genes that allow fireflies and jellyfish to emit light.

In addition, plant researchers are turning to genetic engineering to help plants cope with toxic metals such as cadmium, copper, lead, zinc, and mercury, produced by industry and mining. Scientists have identified genes for metal-resistance proteins that sequester and prevent the absorption of metals. Plants engineered for enhanced expression of these genes can thrive in metal-contaminated soils that would kill normal plants. The next step is to transfer these genes to trees, to reclaim polluted soils.

A Better World

Clearly, genetic engineering is creating entirely new and unprecedented uses of living things. This technology holds great potential to bolster the health, food resources, and economies of all people. Although many hurdles exist, it seems reasonable to suggest that only creative aptitude and motivation limit the terrain to which genetic engineering can be applied.

> *"Biotechnology has much to offer. But, as
> with the introduction of other technological
> innovations throughout history, the final
> costs have yet to be calculated."*

Genetic Engineering May Harm Society

Jeremy Rifkin

Jeremy Rifkin is president of the Foundation on Economic Trends and the author of over a dozen books examining the impact of scientific and technological innovation on society, including *The Biotech Century: Harnessing the Gene and Remaking the World*, from which the following viewpoint was adapted. In it, Rifkin predicts that genetic engineering will ultimately transform society just as the Industrial Revolution did. He doubts that advances in genetic manipulation will be unequivocally beneficial, and warns that most people will welcome the new technologies without considering their potential dangers. He also raises the question of who—scientists, the government, or corporations—will decide how these powerful technologies are used.

As you read, consider the following questions:

1. In the futuristic scenario outlined by biologist Lee Silver, as paraphrased by Rifkin, how will society be divided once the genetic engineering of humans becomes commonplace?
2. According to Rifkin, how do modernist supporters of genetic engineering view nature?
3. What does the author believe is "the most troubling political question in all of human history"?

Excerpted from Jeremy Rifkin, *The Biotech Century*. Copyright ©1998 Jeremy Rifkin. Reprinted with permission from Jeremy P. Tarcher, a division of Penguin Putnam Inc.

While the 20th century was shaped largely by spectacular breakthroughs in the fields of physics and chemistry, the 21st century will belong to the biological sciences. Scientists around the world are quickly deciphering the genetic code of life, unlocking the mystery of millions of years of biological evolution on Earth. As a result of the new breakthroughs in molecular biology and biotechnology, our way of life is likely to be more fundamentally transformed in the next several decades than in the previous thousand years. By the year 2025, we and our children may be living in a world utterly different from anything human beings have ever experienced in the past. Long-held assumptions about nature, including our own human nature, are likely to be rethought. Ideas about equality and democracy are also likely to be redefined, as well as our vision of what is meant by such terms as "free will" and "progress.". . .

Genetic Discrimination

Societies have always been divided between the haves and the have-nots, the powerful and the powerless, the elite and the masses. Throughout history, people have been segregated by caste and class, with myriad rationales used to justify the injustices imposed by the few on the many. Race, religion, language, and nationality are all well-worn methods of categorization and victimization. Now, with the emergence of the genetic revolution, society entertains the prospect of a new and more serious form of segregation. One based on genotype. . . .

Segregating individuals by their genetic makeup represents a fundamental shift in the exercise of power. In a society in which the individual can be stereotyped by genotype, institutional power of all kinds becomes more absolute. At the same time, the increasing polarization of society into genetically "superior" and "inferior" individuals and groups will create a new and powerful social dynamic. Families that can afford to program "superior" genetic traits into their fetuses at conception will ensure their offspring an even greater biological advantage—and thus a social and economic advantage as well. For the emerging "genetic underclass," the issue of genetic stereotyping is likely to lead to growing protests and the birth of a worldwide "genetic rights" movement as an ever-growing number of victims of genetic discrimination organize collectively to demand their right to participate freely and fully in the coming biotech century.

The Gen Rich vs. the Gen Poor

Some genetic engineers envision a future with a small segment of the human population engineered to "perfection," while others remain as flawed reminders of an outmoded evolutionary design. Molecular biologist Lee Silver of Princeton University writes about a not too distant future made up of two distinct biological classes, which he refers to as the "Gen Rich" and the "Naturals." The Gen Rich, who account for 10% of the population, have been enhanced with synthetic genes and have become the rulers of society. They include Gen Rich businesspeople, musicians, artists, intellectuals, and athletes—each enhanced with specific synthetic genes to allow them to succeed in their respective fields in ways not even conceivable among those born of nature's lottery.

At the center of the new genetic aristocracy are the Gen Rich scientists, who are enhanced with special genetic traits that increase their mental abilities, giving them power to dictate the terms of future evolutionary advances on Earth. Silver writes:

> With the passage of time, the genetic distance between Naturals and the Gen Rich has become greater and greater, and now there is little movement up from the Natural to the Gen Rich class. . . . All aspects of the economy, the media, the entertainment industry, and the knowledge industry are controlled by members of the Gen Rich class. . . . In contrast, Naturals work as low-paid service providers or as laborers. . . . Gen Rich and Natural children grow up and live in segregated social worlds where there is little chance for contact between them. . . . [Eventually,] the Gen Rich class and the Natural class will become the Gen Rich humans and the Natural humans—entirely separate species with no ability to crossbreed and with as much romantic interest in each other as a current human would have for a chimpanzee.

Silver acknowledges that the increasing polarization of society into a Gen Rich class and a Natural class might be unfair, but he is quick to add that wealthy parents have always been able to provide all sorts of advantages for their children. "Anyone who accepts the right of affluent parents to provide their children with an expensive private school education cannot use unfairness as a reason for rejecting the use of reprogenetic technologies," Silver argues. Like many of his colleagues, Silver is a strong advocate of the new genetic technologies. "In a society that values human freedom above all else," he writes, "it is hard to find any legitimate basis for restricting the use of reprogenetics."

Difficult Choices

Even with all the excitement being generated around the new genetic technologies, we sense, though dimly, the menacing outline of a eugenics shadow on the horizon. Still, we would find it exceedingly difficult to say no to a technological revolution that offers such an impressive array of benefits. Thus we find ourselves ensnared on the horns of a dilemma as we make the first tentative moves into the biotech century. One part of us, our more ancient side, reels at the prospect of the further desacralizing of life, of reducing ourselves and all other sentient creatures to chemical codes to be manipulated for purely instrumental and utilitarian ends. Our other side, the one firmly entrenched in modernity, is zealously committed to bringing the biology of the planet in line with engineering standards, market forces, and progressive values. Not to proceed with this revolution is unthinkable, as it would violate the very spirit of progress—a spirit that knows no bounds in its restless search to wrest power from the natural world.

Perfecting Nature

The biotech revolution represents the culmination of the Enlightenment vision, a world view that has provided a philosophical and social road map for modern man and woman for more than 200 years. Finding new, more powerful technological ways of controlling and harnessing nature for utilitarian and commercial ends has been the ultimate dream and central motif of the modern age. It was Francis Bacon, the founder of modern science, who urged future generations to "squeeze," "mould," and "shape" nature in order to "enlarge the bounds of human empire to the effecting of all things possible." Armed with the scientific method, Bacon was convinced that we had, at long last, a methodology that would allow us "the power to conquer and subdue" nature and to "shake her to her foundations." Bacon laid the groundwork for the Enlightenment era that followed by providing a systematic vision for humanity's final triumph over nature. Isaac Newton, René Descartes, John Locke, and other Enlightenment philosophers constructed a world view that continues to inspire today's molecular biologists and corporate entrepreneurs in their quest to capture and colonize the last frontier of nature, the genetic commons that is the heart of the natural world.

The biotech century promises to complete the modernists' journey by "perfecting" both human nature and the rest of nature, all in the name of progress. The short-term benefits of the emerging Biotechnological Age appear so impressive that any talk of curtailing or preventing their widespread application is likely to be greeted with incredulity, if not outright hostility. Who could oppose the engineering of new plants and animals to feed a hungry world? Who could object to engineering new forms of biological energy to replace a dwindling reserve of fossil fuels? Who could protest the introduction of new microbes to eat up toxic wastes and other forms of chemical pollution? Who could refuse genetic surgery to eliminate crippling diseases? How could anyone in good conscience oppose a technology that offers such hope for bettering the lot of humanity?

The Benefits of Genetic Engineering

In the years to come, a multitude of new genetic engineering techniques will be forthcoming. Every one of the breakthroughs in biotechnology will be of benefit to someone, under some circumstance, somewhere in society. Each will, in some way, appear to advance the future security of an individual, a group, or society as a whole. The point that needs to be emphasized is that bioengineering is coming to us not as a threat but as a promise, not as a punishment but as a gift. While the thought of engineering living organisms still conjures up sinister images in the movies, it no longer does so in the marketplace. Quite the contrary, what we see before our eyes are not monstrosities but useful products and hopeful futures. We no longer feel dread, but only elated expectation at the great possibilities that lie in store for each of us in the biotech century.

Reprinted with permission from Andy Singer.

For its most ardent supporters, engineering life to improve humanity's own prospects is, no doubt, seen as the highest expression of ethical behavior. Any resistance to the new technology is likely to be castigated by the growing legion of true believers as inhuman, irresponsible, morally reprehensible, and perhaps even criminally culpable.

Who Will Control These New Technologies?

On the other hand, the new genetic engineering technologies raise one of the most troubling political questions in all of human history. To whom, in this new era, would we entrust the authority to decide what is a good gene that should be added to the gene pool and what is a bad gene that should be eliminated? Should we entrust the federal government with that authority? Corporations? The university scientists? From this perspective, few of us are able to point to any institution or group of individuals we would entrust with decisions of such import. If, however, we were asked whether we would sanction new biotech advances that could enhance the physical, emotional, and mental well-being of people, we would not hesitate for a moment to add our support.

We appear caught between our instinctual distrust of the institutional forces that are quickly consolidating their power over the new genetic technologies and our desire to increase our own personal choices and options in the biological marketplace. While control of the new genetic technologies is being concentrated in the hands of scientists, transnational companies, government agencies, and other institutions, the products and services are being marketed under the guise of expanding freedom of choice for millions of consumers.

In the early stages of this new technological and commercial revolution, the informal bargain being struck between the governing institutions of society and consumers appears to be a reasonable one. Biotechnology has much to offer. But, as with the introduction of other technological innovations throughout history, the final costs have yet to be calculated. Granting a specific institution or group of individuals the power to determine a better-engineered crop or animal or a new human hormone seems a trifle in comparison with the potential returns. It is only when one considers the lifetime of the agreement that the full import of the politics of the Biotechnological Age becomes apparent.

A Profound New Ability to Shape the Future

Throughout history, some people have always controlled the futures of other people. Today, the ultimate exercise of power is within our grasp: the ability to control, at the most fundamental level, the future lives of unborn generations by engineering their biology in advance, making them "partial" hostages of their own architecturally designed blueprints. I use the word "partial" because, like many others, I believe that environment is a major contributing factor in determining the course of one's life. It is also true, however, that one's genetic makeup plays a role in helping to shape one's destiny. Genetic engineering, then, represents the power of authorship, albeit "limited" authorship. Being able to engineer even minor changes in the physical and behavioral characteristics of future generations represents a new era in human history. Never before has such power over human life been even a possibility.

Should power of this sort be granted to any public or commercial institution or, for that matter, even to consumers? Whether institutionally motivated or consumer driven, the power to determine the genetic destiny of millions of human beings yet to come lessens the opportunities of every new arrival to shape his or her own personal life story.

Still, at the dawn of the biotech century, the authorial power, though formidable, appears so far removed from any potential threat to individual human will as to be of little concern. Many of us will be eager to take advantage of the new gene therapies, both for ourselves and for our offspring, if they deliver on their promise to enhance our physical, emotional, and mental health. After all, part of the essence of being truly human is the desire to alleviate suffering and enhance human potential.

The problem is that biotechnology has a distinct beginning but no clear end. Cell by cell, tissue by tissue, organ by organ, we might willingly surrender our personhood in the marketplace. In the process, each loss will be compensated for with a perceived gain until there is little left to exchange. It is at that very point that the cost of our agreement becomes apparent. But it is also at that point that we may no longer possess the very thing we were so anxious to enrich: our humanity. In the decades to come, we humans might well barter ourselves away, one gene at a time, in exchange for some measure of temporary well-being. In the end, the personal and collective security we fought so long and hard to preserve may well be irreversibly compromised in pursuit of our own engineered perfection.

> *"[One] type of gene therapy . . . adds*
> *normal genes . . . to produce something*
> *the patient lacks due to genetic defects.*
> *[Another type works] by obstructing genes*
> *that cause disease."*

Advances in Biotechnology Could Help Eliminate Disease

Eric S. Grace

In the following viewpoint, science writer Eric S. Grace explains how scientists hope to use genetic engineering to treat and cure genetic diseases. One promising technique, Grace explains, is gene therapy, which involves using genetically altered blood cells or viruses to introduce new genes into a person's body. Genetically engineering bacteria to produce medicines and using gene splicing techniques to make vaccines safer and more effective are other major areas of research. Crucial to all these techniques, writes Grace, is the Human Genome Project, which is in the process of mapping all human chromosomes. Grace is the author of *Biotechnology Unzipped: Promises and Realities*.

As you read, consider the following questions:

1. How did researchers first use gene therapy to treat adenosine deaminase (ADA), as described by the author?
2. What, according to Grace, are the first, second, and third stages of gene therapy?
3. What does the author say was the first human-produced compound to be produced by bacteria, through the use of genetic engineering?

The Human Genome Project is an ambitious plan to map and sequence all 100,000 or so genes found in human DNA. It is a task that has occupied hundreds of scientists in labs around the world since about 1986.

Know Thyself

The first human genes to be identified, back in the 1970s, were those connected with diseases such as cystic fibrosis. Part of the motivation to sequence the entire genome (that is, all the genes present in a complete set of chromosomes) was the desire to learn more about the genetic roots of disease and to discover more genes that might be used in gene therapy. In 1971, only 15 human genes had been localized to specific chromosomes, most on the easily identified sex chromosome. By the mid-1990s, researchers had mapped the location of about 2,000 genes—an impressive number, but still only 2% of the entire human genome.

The ability to map genes was boosted by the development of recombinant DNA technology—in particular the use of restriction enzymes to cut DNA molecules into small fragments with known endpoints. The restriction enzyme cutting sites act as easily identified markers that let scientists compare different fragments for the presence or absence of particular genes. Bit by bit, they build up collections of fragments that overlap each other in known order until they have eventually spanned the entire length of a chromosome. Adjacent fragments form ordered chromosome libraries that help researchers locate particular genes.

Mapping the location of genes on a chromosome is only the first step. The ultimate aim is to know the sequence of bases in each gene. This is an even lengthier task, since there are about 3 billion base pairs in a set of 23 human chromosomes.

Many scientists found the launch of this huge research program stimulating—like the American drive to put a man on the moon during the 1960s. Reviewing the genome project in 1989, James Trefil, professor of physics at George Mason University, wrote: "It represents nothing less than the ultimate scientific response to the Socratic dictum 'Know Thyself.'" Other scientists were less enthusiastic, seeing much of the exercise as a colossal waste of time, money, and human resources. . . .

The Continuing Story of Gene Therapy

The first actual use of gene therapy began in September 1990, with the treatment of a child suffering from a rare genetic immunodeficiency disease caused by the lack of the enzyme adenosine deaminase (ADA). ADA-deficient people have persistent infections and high risk of early cancer, and many die in their first months of life. The much publicized "bubble boy," David, had this disease. David lived for nine years in a plastic chamber to prevent contact with viruses, which his immune system could not combat.

As with many other genetic disorders, the root of ADA deficiency lies in the body's inability to produce a key chemical because of a defective gene coding. The disease occurs only in children who inherit defective copies of the ADA gene from both parents. A child who inherits a defective copy from one parent and a normal copy from the other will not have the disease, but may pass on the defective copy of the gene to the next generation.

Researchers had identified the normal ADA gene in human white blood cells during the early 1980s. They wanted to see what happened when they introduced copies of this normal gene into a lab culture of T-cells taken from ADA-deficient patients. T-cells were used because they are easy to obtain and grow in the lab, and they are easy to alter genetically.

After ADA genes were transferred into the T-cells by genetically engineered viral vectors, the cells began to produce the ADA enzyme as predicted. The amount of enzyme produced was about 25% of normal, but more than enough to correct the conditions caused by ADA-deficiency. As well, the genetically altered cells had the same life-span as normal T-cells—longer than the life-span of uncorrected T-cells from ADA patients. The beauty of this technique is that the desired gene not only remains in the cell as long as it survives, but it is duplicated and passed on to all the cell's descendants whenever the cells divide.

With the success of the lab experiment, researchers were ready to try out the technique on patients suffering from

ADA-deficiency. The first to be treated was a 4-year-old girl, then, a year later, a 9-year-old. Early results were encouraging for both children. On a regimen of infusion with ADA gene-corrected cells every one or two months, both patients showed normal levels of active T-cells in their blood after a year, and both developed improved immune function.

Somatic Cell vs. Germ Line Gene Therapy

Question: *Why haven't researchers been more successful in using somatic cell gene therapy—replacing defective genes in a patient's tissues with normal versions—to cure genetic diseases such as cystic fibrosis?*

[Molecular biologist Lee M.] Silver: Somatic cell gene therapy is very difficult to do. A living person has millions of cells, and you are trying to get a new gene into a reasonable percentage of those cells to fix a disease like cystic fibrosis. Cystic fibrosis patients have a defective gene that keeps them from making a certain protein. So in theory, if you put the good gene into those cells, they could make the protein. . . . In practice, though, it is very, very difficult to get those genes into a large number of cells. This has always been the case.

However, I should say that whenever I have said that something was hard or impossible, I have been shot down by the advance of science. . . .

What about germ line therapy? Germ line therapy means introducing a gene into an embryo or egg at an early stage of development so that the gene appears in every cell in an animal or person's body. Is germ line gene therapy more feasible than somatic cell therapy?

Silver: Absolutely. Germ line therapy is easy. We have already gotten it to work on lots of different animals. Mice were the first animals in which it was perfected. It has been working on mice now since the 1980s, when the genes for human hemoglobin were put into embryos. Since that time, it has become commonplace and easy to do. My graduate students learn how to do it in their first year. There are tens of thousands of people who can do germ line genetic engineering on animal embryos. And the important thing is that, under the microscope, you can't distinguish a mouse embryo from the human ones. So if you can do it with mice, you can, in principle, do it with humans.

Interview with Lee M. Silver, *Reason*, May 1999.

Because the altered T-cells won't last forever, it wasn't a permanent cure—that would require using bone marrow stem cells. It was a temporary therapy that depends on regular infusion of engineered T-cells. But, like the use of insulin by diabetics, it allowed these patients to lead relatively normal lives. Within a year of her initial treatment, the first little girl was able to attend school, swim, dance, and ice-skate with her family and friends, with no more risk of catching infections than they had.

Blood cells can be genetically altered and reintroduced to the body by a simple injection into a blood vessel. But what if you want to alter genes in the cells of an organ, such as the liver? One approach is to remove a piece of the liver, divide it into individual cells, insert the appropriate genes into each cell, and transplant the engineered cells back into the patient.

A second approach, according to gene-transfer pioneer William French Anderson and others, is to develop smart vectors—ones that can find their own way to diseased tissue inside the body. Rather than inserting genes into cells in petri dishes, we would inject the new generation of vectors directly into patients to carry genes to their targets like guided missiles. This could be achieved by attaching molecules to the vector that recognize specific proteins found on the surface of cells in the target organ.

Gene Therapy to Obstruct Disease

The type of gene therapy I've described adds normal genes to a patient to produce something the patient lacks due to genetic defects. Another type of gene therapy works in a different way, by obstructing genes that cause disease.

In this strategy, called antisense therapy, scientists add a gene that mirrors the target gene—say, one that causes arthritis. The engineered gene produces RNA that complements the RNA of the troublesome gene, binding onto it and blocking its action. So, for example, if the disease-causing gene produces an unwanted protein, antisense therapy will prevent the protein from being formed. If the gene suppresses the formation of a wanted protein, the therapy will allow for normal protein production.

The first stage of gene therapy—identifying genes associated with disease—is fairly well established, thanks to the Human Genome Project. News reports frequently announce the discovery of genes responsible for this or that condition, from Alzheimer's disease to baldness. Research efforts now concentrate on the second and third stages of the process: delivering genes safely to their targets in the body and controlling gene expression in the altered cells. These steps are crucial to gene therapy's success and are likely to take the next 10 to 20 years to develop.

Much of modern medical treatment depends on the use of chemicals, and a large part of the medical biotech industry involves producing large quantities of pure drugs tailored for specific tasks. Some are extracted from natural sources, some are manufactured synthetic compounds, but more and more are produced by engineering cells with recombinant DNA.

The Interferon Story

The first big success story in the commercial production of drugs by genetic engineering was interferon, a naturally occurring compound connected with the immune system.

Discovered in 1957, interferon is produced by cells in the human body in response to viral attack. It promotes production of a protein that stimulates the immune system, interfering with the spread of infection.

Although the usefulness of interferon was recognized at once, it could not be marketed for widespread medical use. The chemical is produced by the body in such tiny amounts that it would take the blood from 90,000 donors to provide only one gram of interferon, and even then the product would be only about 1% pure. In 1978, a single dose of impure interferon cost about $50,000 to obtain.

All that changed dramatically with the birth of genetic engineering. In 1980, Swiss researchers introduced a gene for human interferon into bacteria, the first time such a procedure had been done with human genes. Cloning millions of bacterial cells from the original engineered one, they were then able to produce a cheap and abundant supply of the previously rare protein. By the mid-1980s, supplies had shot up, and pure interferon was being produced for about $1 per dose.

It was an example of the kind of achievement that makes supporters of medical biotechnology so enthusiastic. Interferon is now used not only to combat viral infection in transplant patients, but also to fight other viral diseases (including the common cold), and as an anticancer drug.

Genes and Vaccines

A big advantage of using genetic engineering to produce drugs is that it's possible to mass-produce chemicals that might otherwise be difficult and costly to extract, or simply unavailable by conventional means. Another important advantage is that drugs produced in this way are pure and, if made using human genes, fully compatible with use in people.

For example, before engineered bacteria were cloned to manufacture human insulin, the main source of this hormone (used to treat diabetes) was the pancreas of cattle or pigs. Although similar to human insulin, animal insulin is not identical and causes allergic reactions in some patients. The human protein produced by bacteria with recombinant DNA, however, has no such effect.

To take another example, vaccines against disease are traditionally prepared from killed or "disarmed" pathogens (disease-causing microbes). They are effective in the vast majority of people, but a small percentage of the population have allergic reactions to vaccines. There is also a very small risk of vaccine organisms reactivating to their former pathogenic state. Genetically engineered vaccines are safer because they contain no living organisms—only the proteins that stimulate the body to develop immunity.

Vaccines are the second-largest category of over 200 drugs now being produced by American pharmaceutical companies using biotechnology. Other products include hormones, interferons, blood-clotting factors, antisense molecules, and enzymes. Most of these drugs are still undergoing clinical testing and are designed to combat cancer, AIDS, asthma, diabetes, heart disease, Lyme disease, multiple sclerosis, rheumatoid arthritis, and viral infections.

A Long Way to Go

But the bottom line is that mapping and even sequencing genes is only a beginning. That knowledge alone won't tell us the gene's functions. Of the 2,000 or so genes whose locations are mapped today, we know the functions of only a few hundred. And knowing the functions won't tell us how those functions are actually carried out—how genes are expressed and what the biochemical steps are between the coding for a protein and the symptoms of a disease.

Although advancing knowledge is rapidly closing in on these areas, we needn't worry just yet about having all the secrets of life.

"In the marketplace that we've deified, few moral checks and balances remain. Our great research universities . . . don't want ethical considerations to limit their own biotech royalties."

Advances in Biotechnology Could Be Abused

Jeffrey Klein

In the following viewpoint, Jeffrey Klein, editor-in-chief of *Mother Jones* magazine, argues that the future of genetic engineering will be shaped, for the worse, by the desire to make a profit from genetic research. Klein argues, for example, that while the desire to improve human health is a major goal of gene therapy, people would also pay for a genetic cure for baldness or wrinkles. He also notes that scientists will probably learn how to genetically manipulate embryos before they develop techniques that will introduce new genes into adults. Klein believes that, given the abuse of eugenics in the past, the use of biotechnology for "human breeding" of enhanced embryos would be unethical and potentially dangerous.

As you read, consider the following questions:

1. What three uses does the biotechnology company Geron hope to develop from the cloning of telomerase, according to the author?
2. How did Sir Francis Galton first define the term *eugenics*, according to Klein?
3. What does Klein say is the ultimate goal of start-up biotechnology companies?

Under a microscope in an ordinary-looking lab housed in a nondescript industrial park, I peered at immortal human cells. They looked sleeker than their mortal cousins. At the Geron Corporation, a biotech firm in Menlo Park, California, scientists have apparently discovered how to keep healthy human cells dividing indefinitely. This genetic breakthrough is astonishing, and the long-term consequences are incalculable. When I visited the lab in mid-March, Geron's genetically altered cells had already thrived two-and-a-half times longer than their expected natural life span. And they were still dividing.

Scientists associated with Geron theorized that animal cells are programmed to divide a fixed number of times in their lives, and that these program instructions are coded on the ends of the cells' chromosomes. The ends erode with each cell division; after a preset number of divisions and erosions, cells stop dividing and begin to degrade. A year ago, Geron cloned a gene that produces telomerase, an enzyme that keeps rebuilding the ends of chromosomes. Then the scientists transferred this gene into a young, healthy cell— and, voilà, the cell hasn't stopped dividing, nor has it mutated into a cancerous form.

This breakthrough has a host of potential therapeutic applications, but Geron is focused on three. The first is as a possible cure for cancer. Now that scientists have figured out how to keep cells dividing indefinitely, the flip side could be discovering how to make malignant ones stop. If a cancer cure proves elusive, Geron hopes medical researchers may still be able to use the discovery to treat diseases associated with aging—e.g., retinal decay, hardening of the arteries, osteoporosis. And if all else fails, a fallback revenue plan could be to use this technology to treat wrinkles.

When venture capitalists, pharmaceutical giants, and stockholders have put $118.5 million into your company, you take what you can get as quickly as you can get it. Geron patented the use of telomerase before it knew what the biotechnology might actually be able to do. Prospective patents have been crucial to Geron because the fledgling company was in a frantic race with five other firms to reverse cellular aging and to become a leading player in the new "eugenics revolution."

The Dark History of Eugenics

Walter Funk, the very bright molecular biologist who showed me around Geron, immediately objected to my associating his company's work with the term "eugenics," which he said was based on bad science. Obviously, scientists are wary of a word that conjures up images of the Final Solution. However, the term still offers an apt warning.

Eugenics was first defined in 1883 by English anthropometrist Sir Francis Galton, Darwin's cousin, as the "science of improving the stock." Because it was seen as a cutting-edge science, eugenics took root in America and imparted respectability to exclusionary immigration laws, which limited the entry not just of those with hereditary diseases but of entire ethnic groups, as well. Eugenics even made its way into the Supreme Court, which in 1927 upheld compulsory sterilizations in the case of *Buck v. Bell.* Oliver Wendell Holmes, the most progressive justice of the era, wrote, "Three generations of imbeciles are enough."

Of course, you could argue that Holmes was simply a product of his time. H.H. Goddard, a prominent American researcher, had recently coined the word "moron" to designate "high-grade" mental defectives. Delineating these people by slightly subaverage scores on primitive IQ tests, Goddard judged them to be more dangerous than obvious idiots because their gene pool might proliferate. Goddard favored keeping "morons" happily segregated in colonies where they could be prevented from breeding.

Adolf Hitler praised American eugenics in *Mein Kampf* and convinced his nation that defectives shouldn't just be segregated or sterilized—they should be eradicated. Once the Nazis took the eugenics movement to its extreme, no one dared use the term. After World War II, the University of London renamed its Department of Eugenics as the Department of Human Genetics, and numerous other institutions around the world followed suit. But whether you call it "eugenics" or "human genetics," the impulse is still to upgrade the stock of the human race.

Medical miracle cures are everyone's stated aim, but other modifications are enticing. If we can change an embryo to reduce the possibility of cancer, why shouldn't we simultaneously reduce the possibility of obesity or baldness? We could confidently raise not just a disease-free baby girl, but a little girl with blue eyes and blond hair, likely to grow into a perfectly proportioned woman with an enhanced reasoning capacity.

Misuse of Biotechnology Is Likely

Scenarios like this aren't publicly discussed by budding biotech firms or scientists seeking government grants. America's eagerness to seize the future is shadowed by our fear that the future might seize us. Our businesslike attitude toward the transformation of human nature is punctuated with bursts of hysteria. Few people paid much attention to biotechnology until Dolly. Then, three days after the cloned sheep was introduced to the public, President Clinton asked a panel to consider the expansion of federal powers over human embryo creation. Soon the Senate began debating anti-cloning bills. It didn't matter that the scientist who cloned Dolly has yet to repeat the feat. What mattered was that biotechnology exploded into our consciousness in a Frankensteinian fashion.

The problem is, the biotech revolution is not always going to happen as dramatically—or as publicly. Instead, it's going to come day by day, step by step. Scientists from the University of Colorado discover in pond scum a protozoan that makes large amounts of telomerase; they decode the genetic structure and later find a matching sequence in human DNA. The University of Colorado licenses this discovery to Geron, which rushes to make a human cell momentarily immortal so that the company can secure patents and keep competitors at bay. "We've sewed the [legal] bag pretty tight," Geron's Funk told me. Legal control encourages pharmaceutical giants such as Pharmacia & Upjohn Inc. to sign a $58 million collaboration agreement, which increases the pressure to deliver profits before the patents run out.

Even without pressure from multinational drug companies, American aggressiveness probably would not allow any genetic insight, once gained, to lie fallow. The whole nature of American inventiveness can be summed up by the insidious Nike slogan: "Just Do It." And that results in a mad, government-approved race among biotech companies to patent findings before considering just how corporate control of the human blueprint might affect our species.

The Real Potential for Human Breeding

One characteristic driving Americans to pioneer genetic upgrades is our abiding fear of imperfection. This country was founded on Protestant principles, including the idea of salvation. Many of us keep searching for more impressive ways to prove our internal worth. We're eager to engineer evolution because we're restless with who we are.

Reprinted with permission from Axel Scheffler.

But this drive to enhance our worth will soon present us with a fundamental choice: Should we use biotech for human breeding? Genetic science is more likely to come up with a test that tells which embryos are prone to develop cancer prematurely than it is to come up with a cancer cure. Diagnosing an embryo should prove easier and cheaper than reversing disease in a fully grown adult. Given a choice between fetuses that have perhaps 20 years' difference in their likely life spans, which would you choose?

If the United States bans such practices, richer parents may go to, say, Saudi Arabia. That's where a British doctor recently set up a test-tube clinic that allows sex-selection because the practice is illegal in Great Britain. Those parents who select little Johnny over little Janie because he'll be robust aren't likely to tell their neighbors. Legal and moral complications aside, they'd probably want Johnny's vivacity to be seen as an inevitable reflection of their own virtues.

In fairness, the earnest scientists who are pioneering these genetic breakthroughs don't want their work to be misused. As Funk put the immortalized cells back into their high-tech incubator, he noted that "every dirt-poor village in India has a sonogram" so that parents can distinguish boys from girls and get rid of the latter. Before he came to Geron, Funk was a graduate student in a lab that sampled placentas in order to tell parents with a history of hemophilia whether their in utero children carried the disease. But, he was quick to add, "no one ever had an abortion." They used the information, he said, solely to ensure that all medical precautions would be taken for a safe hospital delivery.

Of course, if you were considering aborting a hemophiliac child, would you inform the test lab?

The Profit Motive Drives Biotechnology

Laboratory scientists can't be expected to question progress closely. A few years ago, I did some reporting at Lawrence Livermore Lab in California, one of three U.S. nuclear weapons facilities. Almost all the physicists and engineers I met believe they are perfecting nuclear weapons for the good of mankind. Given the absence of a superpower enemy, the more apparent reason these scientists persist is because they love their field. Lawrence Livermore has an elaborate, color-coded security system; barbwire enclaves restrict access even inside of highly classified zones. The highest status, however, is awarded not for the greatest access. Rather, you enter the most select club when one of your bomb designs makes it all the way to a test detonation.

Most biotechnologists want to set off their own version of the big one. Biotech startups have an equally naked drive: They want to show enough profit potential to be bought out by the multinational pharmaceuticals. And these big boys simply want to stimulate consumer demand and control markets, whatever the consequences. In the marketplace that we've deified, few moral checks and balances remain. Our great research universities, for example, don't want ethical considerations to limit their own biotech royalties.

Does the nature of such seekers influence the outcome of the search? Yes. Character is as powerful as DNA in the shaping of destiny. A cure for cancer would be astonishing, but do we really want to experiment with a genetic solution for wrinkles? What is this agelessness that we yearn for so badly, except a desire to escape the weight of our history and experience?

From the pond comes another primal insight. In Greek mythology, Narcissus is so beautiful that he is unable to love anyone else. Instead, seeing his image reflected in a still pool, he falls in love with it. But all his efforts to touch, to caress, to embrace that reflection cause it to distort and disappear. Unable to relinquish the image of his own perfection, Narcissus dwindles into the narcissus flower we know today. Since he lacked the ability to embrace those creatures he deemed less perfect, the gods moved him down the chain of being.

Three or four generations from now, elites may have been genetically reshaped through selective breeding. Will these new people be grateful for the characteristics we picked? Or will they feel divorced from us in some undefinable way? Perhaps their longing for old-fashioned connectedness will be tinged with contempt. They may contend that we didn't transform human nature primarily for their sake, but for our own vanity.

Periodical Bibliography

The following articles have been selected to supplement the diverse views presented in this chapter. Addresses are provided for periodicals not indexed in the *Readers' Guide to Periodical Literature*, the *Alternative Press Index*, the *Social Sciences Index*, or the *Index to Legal Periodicals and Books*.

Ronald Bailey	"Liberation Biology," *Reason*, May 1999.
John Carey	"'We Are Now Starting the Century of Biology,'" *Business Week*, August 24, 1998.
Fred Edwords	"How Biotechnology Is Transforming What We Believe and How We Live," *Humanist*, September/October 1999.
Stephen S. Hall	"Biotech on the Move," *Technology Review*, November/December 1999.
Walter Isaacson	"The Biotech Century," special section, *Time*, January 11, 1999.
Mother Jones	Special biotechnology report, May/June 1998.
David Shenk	"Biocapitalism: What Price the Genetic Revolution?" *Harper's Magazine*, December 1997.
James Shreeve	"Secrets of the Gene," *National Geographic*, October 1999.
Gary Stix	"Dark Prophet of Biogenetics: Jeremy Rifkin," *Scientific American*, August 1997.
Craig Ventner and Daniel Cohen	"The Twenty-First Century: The Century of Biology," *New Perspectives Quarterly*, special issue, 1997.

CHAPTER 2

Is the Genetic Engineering of Humans Ethical?

Chapter Preface

Many people flatly oppose the genetic engineering of humans. Whether from a religious or secular perspective, they argue that interfering with "the building blocks of life," as DNA is often described, could have dangerous, unexpected consequences and should not be done. Other observers accept that scientists now have the technology to genetically engineer humans and will eventually use it. In their view, the question is not whether genetic engineering will be applied to humans, but how.

The least controversial proposed use of human genetic engineering is the elimination of genetic disorders. Yet gene therapy techniques could be used for more than just treating disease. Biochemistry professor W. French Anderson, one of the pioneers of gene-based therapy, raises these concerns about his own research: "Once we have the ability to give a patient any gene we want in order to treat a disease, then we will also have the ability to give a human being genes for any purpose besides therapy. . . . The temptation to try to use genes . . . to improve ourselves is very strong—maybe even irresistible." Anderson concludes that genetic engineering of humans should be limited to the treatment of serious disease, and that genetic enhancement—the use of genetic engineering to, for example, cure baldness, improve intelligence, or increase the human lifespan—should be off-limits.

However, molecular biologist Lee M. Silver, in his book *Remaking Eden: Cloning and Beyond in a Brave New World*, embraces the prospect of enhancing humans through genetic manipulation. Moreover, he rejects the distinction between treating disease and "enhancing": "It is impossible to draw a line in an objective manner. In every instance, genetic engineering will be used to add something to a child's genome that didn't exist in the genomes of either of its parents. Thus, in every case, genetic engineering will be genetic enhancement."

The prospect of genetically enhancing children has raised some of the most controversial questions in the debate over genetic engineering. The authors in this chapter examine this issue and explore other ways in which the genetic engineering of humans might be used or abused.

"[Genetic engineering is] unnatural . . . but it is not bad."

Genetic Engineering of Humans Is Ethical

Oliver Morton

In the following viewpoint, Oliver Morton argues that the genetic engineering of humans may be "unnatural," but it is not immoral. Rather than rejecting the ability to manipulate nature via genetic engineering, Morton contends, society should embrace it. He maintains that the genetic engineering of humans will simply give parents more choices about what their children will be like; it is how parents make those choices, not biotechnology itself, that is morally relevant. Oliver Morton is a contributing editor at *Wired* magazine.

As you read, consider the following questions:

1. What example from the 1950s does Morton use to show how the Yuk factor is eventually overcome?
2. What example does the author use to show that doctors and scientists are already capable of changing the way genetic information is processed?
3. In the author's opinion, how can the practice of "genotype choice" be prevented from being corrupted into a form of eugenics?

Excerpted from Oliver Morton, "Overcoming Yuk," *Wired*, January 1998. Reprinted with permission from the author.

We might as well start with Dolly. The past five years have seen plenty of other breakthroughs, from bacterial genome sequences to headless frogs, but none has had quite the same impact as the little woolly clone. Maybe that's because, in an odd way, we were prepared for her. Unlike homeotic genes, or DNA hybridization arrays, or secondary cellular messengers, or most of the rest of the stuff of the new biology, cloning is something we think we understand. And there's something deeply emblematic about it, too. Inasmuch as she's just another sheep, Dolly's completely natural; inasmuch as she's a clone of one particular other sheep, she's utterly unnatural. So there she stands, nature and artifice wrapped up into one bundle. Welcome to the future. Ecce ovo. Baaa.

The fact that she was a clone was actually not the most interesting thing about Dolly. Being able to xerox single creatures is not a particularly interesting skill in most circumstances. The important thing about Dolly is that a nucleus was taken from a cell in a laboratory test tube and put into an egg. Manipulating the genes of cells in laboratories is something molecular biologists are getting better and better at. The Dolly technique means that these manipulated genes can now be slotted into eggs much more precisely. From the laboratory and the clinic, the new biology is now poised to move into the field, or the barnyard, or the home. The first practical applications will be sheep with valuable proteins in their milk. Then there may be pigs that make organs for transplanting into humans. Then pets with engaging predetermined characters and advertising logos growing in their fur.

The Yuk Factor

The first of those two applications is pretty widely acceptable. The second is still disgusting to many. It falls prey to what Tom Wilkie, who runs the biomedical ethics section of the Wellcome Trust in London, calls "the Yuk factor." The Yuk factor governs the initial public response to almost every biomedical advance that can easily be understood as being unnatural. Women giving birth after 60? Yuk! Pigs as organ donors? Yuk!

The Yuk factor feels instinctual, primal, a law of nature.

Yet it can pass quite quickly. Take the cornea. In the 1950s it was against the law in Britain to save a patient's sight by grafting a dead person's corneas onto the patient's eyes. This was not just a legal oversight; people found the idea quite deeply Yuk, and it took a prolonged journalistic campaign to get the law changed. (Every contact lens wearer goes through the same process on a personal level. At first there is a definite Yuk to touching the eye; soon it becomes utterly commonplace.)

The Yuk factor boils down to a disgust at what seems unnatural. As we live with the unnatural, though, we begin first to accommodate it, then to accept it, then to appreciate it. That's just as well, because our success as a species rests on ever greater unnaturalness. Sheep were a product of our willingness to disregard nature long before we started cloning them, bred as they were for wool, for mutton, for a willingness to be herded. And what we do to sheep is nothing compared to what we're willing to do to ourselves with the help of qualified doctors and pharmaceutical prowess. The Yuks that surround the new biology reflect its ability to take our unnaturalness to hitherto impossible heights; but our enthusiasm for medicine will overcome them.

"Unnatural" Is Not the Same as "Immoral"

Biology, after all, is about life, not nature. It's just an accident of history that, until recently, everything alive was more or less natural. Nature is a record of 4 billion years of life's successes, written in the language of the genes. Biology's new strength comes from being able to read that record; cracking the genetic code has ushered in one of those wonderful eras of scientific progress when new discoveries keep leading to new techniques with which yet more discoveries can be made. From the ability to splice genes comes the monoclonal antibodies that recognize proteins, the DNA amplifiers that pick up genetic signals previously inaudible, the probes that tell one gene from another, the techniques for making mutations ever more subtle and specific. What used to be a Nobel Prize–worth of research is now a couple of months of PhD drudgery; what PhDs used to do with pride is now done by robots with efficiency. The past five years have seen the knowledge machines blur into ever faster productivity.

That knowledge is beginning to be put to use in unnatural wonders all around the world. There's Dolly. There are millions of other genetically engineered animals, and countless billions of cells in culture, some of them pumping out life-giving medicines under the auspices of biotechnology companies. There's a young woman named Louise Brown [the first test tube baby], and thousands of children created through in vitro fertilization after her. There's a girl called Ashanti DeSilva who was the first child to be deliberately infected with a virus that was supposed to knit a new gene into her cells. And this is all just the beginning.

It's unnatural; it's Yuk; but it is not bad. The natural has no special moral status; it merely has a practical pedigree. That which is natural has the advantage of having been shown to work, and we should bear that in mind. But no gene ever knew what would work in advance, or applied itself to a greater purpose than its own replication; the choices recorded in the genome are not moral choices. Morality has only now come to the genome, because only now is the genome open to deliberate action by people with foresight and responsibility. We can choose life in ways nature could not. But we should not be bound by it.

The Power to Change Nature

Humanity is used to power over nature. Physics has given us abilities that most of our ancestors would have reserved for the gods; the power to visit new worlds, to end this one, to see everything, and to be heard everywhere. All this in barely a hundred years. Biological power will bring changes as profound—and choices with consequences as grave. Unfortunately, most people do not understand that these choices are becoming increasingly possible; they see nature as a set of bonds they cannot break.

The material basis of human nature is more widely accepted today than ever before, largely due to the new biology. The mind has been dissected; thoughts have been imaged; moods are altered. At an intellectual level, human nature, long exiled by social theorists, has made a comeback. To think of the mind as an evolved organ, its patterns of thought as biological as the metabolic pathways of the liver, is now to be at the vanguard of what is called evolutionary psychology, a field that over the past five years has grown from the obsession of a few to the intellectual fashion of many. While its findings may sometimes be fallacious, its foundations are clearly true: If the mind was not shaped by God, then it was shaped by evolution and culture.

Parents Have the Right to Genetically Modify Their Children-to-Be

There are those who will argue that parents don't have the right to control the characteristics of their children-to-be [through genetic engineering]. But American society, in particular, accepts the rights of parents to control every other aspect of their children's lives from the time they are born until they reach adulthood. If one accepts the parental prerogative after birth, it is hard to argue against it before birth, if no harm is caused to the children who emerge.

Many think that it is inherently unfair for some people to have access to technologies that can provide advantages while others, less well-off, are forced to depend on chance alone. I would agree. It is inherently unfair. But once again, American society adheres to the principle that personal liberty and personal fortune are the primary determinants of what individuals are allowed and able to do. Anyone who accepts the right of affluent parents to provide their children with an expensive private school education cannot use "unfairness" as a reason for rejecting the use of reprogenetic technologies.

Lee M. Silver, *Remaking Eden: Cloning and Beyond in a Brave New World*, 1997.

Add to this a misleading way of talking about genetics that involves tagging genes with the problem that accompanies their dysfunction—genes "for" obesity, aggression, dyslexia, and addiction, and their more obviously medical cousins, the genes "for" cancer, Alzheimer's, and high cholesterol—and you get a world where people begin to think that their genes hold road plans for their lives. That their nature controls them.

But the organism is not specified by its genes as a car is specified by its blueprints; it is always already a work in progress. A living being is an information processor that continuously remakes itself, an interaction between matter and information in which neither can take priority. It is a dance of form and substance, of nature and nurture, of matter and information.

At the moment we know a lot about data in our genes, because we recently learned how to read it. We know far less about the processes that use that data to make cells, organs, behaviors, people. That means that, at the moment, people can be faced with the dilemma of knowledge that brings with it little power; they can know they face an increased risk of breast cancer thanks to a faulty gene, thanks to a recently developed test, but not know what to do with that knowledge.

This is a temporary problem. There is every reason to think that we can develop ever subtler ways to change the environment—the social environment, the global environment, the environment in our guts or our blood or our brainstem. And so we can change the way the genetic information is processed.

In some cases we already know how to do this. There is a genetic defect called phenylketonuria (PKU) that disrupts the ability to metabolize the amino acid phenylalanine. Left to itself, it leads to severe mental retardation; in that much, it is a gene "for" imbecility. These days, though, it is not left to itself. In America and much of the rest of the world, every newborn child is tested for PKU, and those who have it are then put on a special diet, one low in phenylalanine. The diet is not pleasant, and sticking with it is hard (it may become easier when cows are engineered to produce phenylalanine-free milk, a development project already under way). But stick with the diet and the child can develop pretty normally. Knowing about nature lets you change nurture to match. The two can be made to mesh.

PKU is a somewhat simple example. But the principle it embodies is one that should guide us through all the new knowledge and pseudo-knowledge about human nature and the workings of the mind that biology is producing at ever greater rates. Knowing the score is the first step toward putting the process back on the rails. Knowledge about genes is the beginning, not the end—the point from which you can start making choices about how to shape your world.

Genetic Engineering vs. Genotype Choice

Addressing a conference at Caltech a few years ago, physicist and science fiction author Gregory Benford imagined the perplexity of historians 50 years hence. "They'll look back at our abortion debates and they'll laugh; they won't see how we could get so worked up about such a simple choice when their biological choices are far, far more complex."

Perhaps the biggest choices will be about children. Better environments tailored for their genes are one thing; but what about better genes, too? Wholesale engineering of human children seems unlikely, for a range of practical, social, and ethical reasons to do with creating human life as an experiment. Much more likely is widespread "genotype choice"—a sort of decentralized, do-it-yourself eugenics.

A couple goes to a clinic and provides some sperm and some eggs. The clinic turns them into embryos and analyzes the different mixtures of the parents' genes each embryo carries. The parents are given the embryos' genetic profiles and advice on how the genes relate to various traits, both physical and mental, in various different conditions. At present, such a profile would be expensive and crude, capable of spotting genes for serious genetic disabilities but not much more. But with better DNA-analysis tools and much more knowledge about which genes do what—both fields that are growing exponentially—the pictures will get sharper and sharper. The parents choose the profile they like, on whatever criteria appeal to them; the chosen embryo is grown a bit further in the test tube, a few cells are snipped out to provide tissue for repairs in later life, and then the pregnancy gets under way. No engineering; just choice.

Many people, including some of the scientists who have made it possible, see this as unethical, the creation of a life as a commodity. Yet people create lives for self-centered purposes—such as support in old age—all the time. Genotype choice would undoubtedly be deeply unnatural. But so is birth in a hospital, not to mention contraception. It would give parents a real power over the sort of people their children will turn out to be. But parents have that power already, to a large degree—through attitudes, affection, and school choice.

A Matter of Individual Choice

Eugenics—the favoring of the reproduction of some genes over others—has a vile history. If genotype choice were to be in the hands of the state, it would likely be a continuation of that history, and a thing to fear and reject. But there is no need for it to be in the hands of the state, and every reason to fight against any strict control the state might try to exercise. Genotype choice should be a matter for individuals, a personal choice about what sort of life they want their children to have.

There would be effects beyond the level of the individual in such a world, as various traits became more common. Symmetrical features would seem a good bet, along with strong immune systems and some types of intelligence. Judging by personal ads, a gene for a good sense of humor would spread like wildfire. Severe genetic disorders would disappear. None of these is clearly a bad thing. Perhaps the most worrying potential by-product of genotype choice would be a skewed sex ratio—and that is already upon us. In India, China, and other countries, ultrasound imaging has led to the preferential abortion of female fetuses on quite a large scale. What can be done about this, though, is not clear. Sex tests are easy enough for a black market to spring up easily; so is abortion. It may be that the only thing to do is to proselytize for women's rights, to convince people that a girl is as valuable as a boy. And to remember that over time, if sex selection swings a long way in one direction, it is bound to swing back. . . .

Choices and Crossroads

It's a happy coincidence of iconography that the double helix was a medical icon long before the discovery of DNA. The two twisted snakes of the caduceus have been with doctors since Hippocrates, as the sacred symbol of Mercury, god of messages, of choices, of crossroads.

Now medicine can offer us more than ever before; more benefits and more choices. Better biology will not solve everything. Warding off many forms of cancer will not make the world perfect; nor will delaying the onset of Alzheimer's by a few decades, or even a century. Better understanding of the relief of emotional suffering will not make us all happy, and new techniques for maximizing the power of the intellect will not make everyone an Einstein. But the past five years suggest that all these things are conceivable over the next century—I'd say quite likely. We need to face them, decide how much we want them, look at ways we can spread their benefits widely, look at what they might cost us.

Nature has been making choices for 4 billion years; every base in the human genome is a result of those natural selections, just as every byte of a computer program is a choice between yes and no. This record has given us our knowledge, but it is no guide to how to use it. Those choices must be made not on the basis of what has worked before—which is all nature can ever offer us—but on the basis of what we want, individually and collectively. From now on the caduceus is ours.

So are the crossroads.

"There is insufficient potential benefit to justify any human genetic engineering."

Genetic Engineering of Humans Is Largely Unethical

Bernard Gert

Bernard Gert is the Eunice and Julian Cohen Professor for the Study of Ethics and Human Values at Dartmouth College. In the viewpoint that follows, he argues that because the potential dangers of genetically engineering humans outweigh the risks, the practice cannot be ethically justified. Gert accepts the use of gene therapy to modify defective tissues in the body, but objects to the genetic engineering of entire humans, since the changes made would be passed onto future generations. In his view, the risk that a harmful gene could be added to the gene pool is too great. In addition, Gert contends that genetic engineering could be used by the wealthy to genetically enhance their children and give them an unfair advantage.

As you read, consider the following questions:
1. How does Gert use the example of diabetes to argue that gene therapy is morally acceptable?
2. How does the author differentiate between negative and positive eugenics?
3. How might genetic engineering be abused by individuals with wealth and power, according to Gert?

Reprinted from Bernard Gert, "Genetic Engineering: Is It Morally Acceptable?" *USA Today Magazine*, January 1999. Reprinted with permission from *USA Today Magazine*.

G enetic engineering involves directly altering the genetic structure of an organism to provide it with traits deemed useful or desirable by those doing the altering. Genetic engineering of plants and animals has been going on since the 1970s, though attempts to introduce such traits through selective breeding has been going on for centuries.

The most straightforward use of genetic engineering involves producing a plant or animal with "improved" characteristics. In the case of agriculture, for example, genetic engineering has produced crop plants resistant to lower temperatures, herbicides, and insect attack, as well as tomatoes with a longer shelf life. A completely different type of genetic engineering involves transplanting a gene, usually human, from one species to another in order to produce a useful product. A patent already has been applied for to mix human embryo cells with those from a monkey or ape to create an animal that might have kidneys or a liver more suitable for transplantation to human beings. There seem to be no limits to the creatures made possible by genetic engineering—e.g., creating edible birds and mammals with minimal brain functions, including no consciousness, so as to avoid protests about the cruelty involved in raising and killing conscious animals for food.

Gene Therapy Has Not Been Controversial

Although particular instances of genetic engineering of plants and animals have caused some controversy, mostly because of environmental or health concerns, genetic engineering is a generally accepted practice. The major moral controversy concerns whether to allow directly altering the genetic structure of human beings. Genetic engineering done by altering the somatic cells of an individual in order to cure genetic and non-genetic diseases has not been controversial. Indeed, what is known as somatic cell gene therapy is becoming a standard method for treating both kinds of diseases. Unlike the genetic engineering used in plants and animals, somatic cell gene therapy alters only the genetic structure of the individual who receives it; the altered genetic structure is not passed on to that individual's offspring. However, now that large mammals such as cows and sheep can be cloned, it may be possible that genetic engineering done by altering somatic cells in human beings may be passed on to future generations of human beings.

Presently, somatic cell genetic engineering is limited to therapy—there has not even been a proposal to use it for enhancement. Clinical trials using human patients have demonstrated the feasibility of somatic cell gene therapy in humans, successfully correcting genetic defects in a large number of cell types. In principle, there is no important moral distinction between injecting insulin into a diabetic's leg and injecting the insulin gene into a diabetic's cells.

Gene Therapy vs. Genetic Enhancement

The most serious moral controversy concerns the application to human beings of the kind of genetic engineering used on plants and animals. This type of human genetic engineering, usually referred to as germ line gene therapy, is regarded by some as the best means to correct severe hereditary defects such as thalassemia, severe combined immune deficiency, or cystic fibrosis. Many believe, though, that genetic engineering to treat or eliminate serious genetic disorders—the practice of negative eugenics—will lead to the process being directed toward enhancing or improving humans, or positive eugenics. This slippery slope argument presupposes that there is something morally unacceptable about positive eugenics, but that has not been shown. No one yet has provided a strong theoretical argument demonstrating that genetic engineering to produce enhanced size, strength, intelligence, or increased resistance to toxic substances is morally problematic.

Eugenics properly has a bad connotation because, prior to the possibility of genetic engineering, eugenics only could be practiced by preventing those who were regarded as having undesirable traits from reproducing. Genetic engineering allows for positive eugenics without limiting the freedom of anyone. The moral force of the objection that genetic engineering, especially positive eugenics or genetic enhancement, is "playing God" is that we do not know that there are no risks. A proper humility and recognition of limited human knowledge and fallibility is required for reliable moral behavior. A strong argument for concluding that genetic enhancement and perhaps even genetic therapy is morally unacceptable is that it risks great harm for many in future generations in order to provide benefits for a few in this one.

Arguments Against Eugenics

Two standard arguments have been put forward that even negative eugenics should not be practiced. The first is that it will result in the elimination of those deleterious alleles (alternate forms of a gene) which may be of some future benefit to the species. The argument is that the genetic variation of a species affords evolutionary plasticity or potential for subsequent adaptation to new and perhaps unforeseen conditions. To eliminate a deleterious mutant allele, like those responsible for cystic fibrosis or sickle cell anemia, could have some risk. It generally is agreed that the recessive gene responsible for sickle cell anemia evolved as an adaptive response to malaria.

This argument is false for two different reasons. The first concerns the nature of genetic maladies. For those based on the inheritance of recessive alleles, it is not the presence of two mutant alleles that causes the malady, but the absence of a normal allele. As long as a normal allele is present, the mutant ones do not cause a genetic disorder. In the case of sickle cell anemia, gene therapy for recessive disorders will work, even though the mutant and non-functional alleles remain. When it is possible not merely to add a gene, but to replace a non-functional mutant allele, the latter no longer will remain. No evolutionary problem is caused by eliminating dominant genes that cause serious genetic disorders such as Huntington's disease.

Almost all genetic disorders are caused by recessive genes, and it seems quite unlikely that there will be any serious attempt to eradicate these genes from the human gene pool, even if it becomes possible and desirable. The technology required must be applied on an individual basis with rather limited accessibility. Because it is a surgical procedure, germ line gene therapy would be done in a medical setting and on a voluntary basis. Although many couples might qualify for gene therapy, just a small number likely would elect to participate. For example, if germ line gene therapy involving gene replacement could be developed for Tay Sachs and was used to treat all embryos showing the disease, the frequency of the Tay Sachs allele in the entire population merely would decrease from 0.0100 to 0.0099 over a generation.

RUNAWAY TRAIN

Reprinted with permission from Kirk Anderson.

The second argument is an iatrogenic (produced inadvertently in a medical procedure) one. The claim is that, since it is impossible to draw a non-arbitrary line that distinguishes positive from negative eugenics by defining what a genetic disorder is, genetic therapy may cause more serious maladies in future generations than it prevents for the present one. However, genetic conditions like hemophilia, cystic fibrosis, and muscular dystrophy all share features common to other serious diseases or disorders, such as cancer. An objective and culture-free distinction can be made between genetic conditions that everyone counts as diseases or disorders and those that no one does. Even if there are some borderline conditions, it is theoretically possible to limit genetic engineering to those conditions about which there is no disagreement. The topic of what counts as a malady—in particular, what counts as a genetic malady—is important for it may affect not only what conditions will be covered by medical insurance, but which ones are suitable for gene therapy. If genetic engineering is used just to cure serious genetic maladies such as Tay Sachs, it is extremely unlikely that more serious genetic maladies will be created in the future.

Genetic Engineering Could Harm Future Generations

While there is no theoretical reason for not using germ line gene therapy, there is a persuasive argument which concludes that all forms of germ line genetic engineering involving humans should be prohibited. This argument, similar to the one against genetic enhancement, claims that even genetic therapy risks great harm for many in future generations, and that there is not sufficient harm prevented to justify these risks. Genetic therapy, like genetic enhancement, not only is permanent during the entire lifetime of the affected individual, the transgene becomes inheritably transmitted to countless members of future generations.

New facts about basic genetic phenomena are being discovered—e.g., five human genetic disorders have been found that are based on mutations involving expandable and contractible trinucleotide repeats. This baffling and novel mechanism for producing mutations was unpredicted, and there currently is no complete explanation for its cause. Similarly, geneticists have discovered another novel and unpredicted phenomenon—genetic imprinting. For a small, but significant, fraction of genes, in humans and other species, the expression of the gene during early embryonic development varies according to its paternal or maternal origin. The biological role of imprinting and the molecular mechanism responsible for selective gene expression remain mysteries. Nevertheless, the effect of genetic imprinting and trinucleotide expansion may be critical in terms of carrying out germ line gene therapy. Problems might not be discovered until the third or fourth generation. Moreover, it seems likely that unpredicted future facts about basic genetic phenomena will be discovered which carry similar risks.

Given even this small possibility of significant harm to many, an analysis of risks and benefits indicates that germ line gene therapy would be justified just in cases of severe maladies, and then only if there were no less radical way of preventing them from occurring. Pre-implantation genetic screening, whereby embryos first are produced by in vitro fertilization, does provide such an alternative. At an early blastocyst stage of development, when the embryo is at the eight- or 16-cell stage, a single embryonic cell is removed and screened, genetically, for the presence of defective alleles. If analysis reveals that the fetus would develop a severe genetic malady, the embryo would not be implanted. If the embryo has no severe genetic malady, uterine implantation would be carried out so that normal development could occur.

Pre-implantation screening can eliminate essentially all severe genetic maladies that could be eliminated by genetic engineering. For those with religious or metaphysical beliefs that prohibit destroying any fertilized human egg, it should be pointed out that genetic engineering usually involves creating more fertilized eggs than one plans to use, since implanting of any fertilized egg, including a genetically altered one, often is not successful.

Consequently, pre-implantation screening eliminates the need for germ line gene therapy. The number of cases whereby both parents carry the genes for a rare deleterious recessive allele, such as cystic fibrosis, are microscopically small. Genetic engineering, then, is necessary only for improving or enhancing people by adding new genes for strength, intelligence, or resistance to pathogens or toxins. Genetic engineering to add improvements, rather than to eliminate defects, may give rise to serious social and political problems.

Genetic Enhancement Would
Lead to Inequality and Abuse

Moreover, gene therapy will be, for the foreseeable future, a very expensive procedure, so only the wealthy will be able to afford it. Germ line gene therapy probably comes as close as is humanly possible to guaranteeing that those families who can afford it will be able to perpetuate their social and political dominance. Thus, together with cloning, it may give rise to a genetically stratified society, as envisioned in Aldous

Huxley's novel, *Brave New World*. Once this technology is well-developed, it can be used by societies in which those in power are not governed by ethical restraints. Individuals may be genetically engineered to provide various tasks—e.g., as warriors. Imagine a group of people engineered to be resistant to various poisonous gases. Still, these concerns, although genuine, are speculative.

On the other hand, scientists know from experience that cutting-edge technology generates pressures for its use. Consequently, it is likely that, if genetic engineering were permitted, the technology would be utilized inappropriately, employed even when a comparable outcome could be accomplished using a less risky method. There is justified concern that genetic engineering advocates will make claims that the risks are less than they really are and the benefits are greater than will be realized. It is at least disconcerting that proponents of germ line gene therapy do not talk at all of the far less risky alternative of pre-implantation screening.

If every scientist, administrator, and venture capitalist involved in applying and commercializing genetic engineering were appropriately thoughtful, there would be much less reason to prohibit development and application for those rare cases in which it could be the therapy of choice. However, based on the cited risks, there is insufficient potential benefit to justify any human genetic engineering. Until certain knowledge of the real risks and benefits associated with human genetic engineering has been obtained, the potential risks to all of the future descendants of the patient outweigh any benefit to a very small number of persons who might benefit. In the event of an unanticipated harmful outcome of genetic engineering using mice or corn, the transgenic organisms can be killed, but clearly this option can not be used with humans.

It takes just a few scientists who have convinced themselves that they know the risks are imaginary and the benefits are real for human genetic engineering to become a field in which researchers compete to be first. National and international recognition, prizes, awards, patents, grants, and other measures of status, wealth, and power are potent incentives to overstate successes and benefits, take unacceptable risks, and dismiss valid objections. The extraordinary loyalty of scientists to one another, resulting in their reluctance to interfere with any research project that their colleagues wish to pursue, makes it very likely that some misguided projects will be carried out.

Technology can not justifiably be used to provide benefits to only a few, even if such benefits are great. In cases where no great harm is being prevented and a large number of people may be put at significant risk, caution must prevail. Even if there is no chance of completely stopping germ line gene therapy, it may be possible to delay it long enough that the technology is developed that enables scientists to repair a gene, rather than replace it. Similarly, it might have been better if the building of nuclear power plants had been delayed until they were designed so that there would be virtually no chance of a nuclear explosion. Indeed, it might have been better to postpone building them until acceptable plans for disposing of nuclear wastes had been developed.

Genetic Engineering Should Be Limited to Genetic Repair

The Human Genome Project involves mapping the entire genome—that is, showing where each gene is located, not only which chromosome it is on, but where on that chromosome. This project was sold to Congress in a somewhat misleading way, its proponents claiming that, by finding the genes responsible for major genetic maladies like cystic fibrosis, as well as those that provide dispositions for standard maladies like cancer and heart disease, scientists better would be able to prevent and cure these conditions. That was true, but the whole Human Genome Project was not needed for this purpose. Most scientists were not so optimistic about it, and there was difficulty in lobbying Congress to appropriate all that money. The solution was to pick just those scientists who were on the optimistic fringe to testify before Congress.

The Human Genome Project also involves sequencing each gene—that is, showing how it is built up out of the base pairs that make up a gene. Most defective genes involve a change in a few of these base pairs, often merely one. Gene repair involves changing the base pair causing the problem. This form of genetic engineering has far less potential for disaster or misuse than the kind being considered. Further, the concept of gene repair reinforces the difference between gene therapy and gene enhancement. It would be inappropriate to regard making any change in a gene as repairing it unless that gene is both different from the standard form and results in some genetic malady. Limiting human genetic engineering to the repairing of genes dramatically would lessen the risks of such engineering while not preventing any of its therapeutic benefits.

Application of common moral reasoning to the question of human genetic engineering—both gene therapy and genetic enhancement—thus seems to lead to a natural solution. The present lack of knowledge should restrict genetic engineering to genetic repair. Such a limitation allows the prevention of all the evils of more expansive forms of genetic engineering while not incurring any of the risks. Given this alternative, allowing any more expansive form of genetic therapy or genetic enhancement does not seem morally acceptable.

"As the practice of prenatal genetic testing expands . . . the total number of abortions will increase, perhaps dramatically."

Genetic Screening Is Ethically Problematic

Ted Peters

Ted Peters is a professor of theology and the author of *For the Love of Children: Genetic Technology and the Future of the Family*, from which the following viewpoint is adapted. In it, Peters describes how advances in genetic research could lead to genetic discrimination, as employers and medical insurers make decisions about people based on their genes. He warns that as doctors become better able to test fetuses for genetic abnormalities, parents will be more and more tempted to terminate pregnancies that might not result in a "perfect" baby. In making decisions about genetic screening and abortion, he concludes, parents must carefully weigh the desire to prevent a child's suffering from genetic disease against the temptation to enhance a child's genetic makeup.

As you read, consider the following questions:

1. In what percent of cases does prenatal genetic testing reveal the presence of a severe genetic disorder, according to Peters?
2. In the author's view, how will an increase in selective abortion affect people living with disabilities?
3. What is the author's view of the genetic selection of sperm or ova, as opposed to a fertilized zygote?

The triumphs of genetic research include the discovery of disease-related genes. The gene for cystic fibrosis, for example, has been found on chromosome 7. Huntington's chorea was discovered lurking on the end of chromosome 4. Inherited breast cancer was traced to chromosome 17, early-onset Alzheimer's disease to chromosome 14 and colon cancer to chromosome 2. Disposition to muscular dystrophy, sickle-cell anemia and 5,000 or more other diseases is being tracked to genetic origins. The search goes on as well for the DNA switches that turn such genes on and off, and for genetic therapies that will turn the bad genes off and keep the good genes on. Such discoveries could improve medical diagnosis, prevention and therapy, thus advancing the quality of health for everyone.

Genetic Discrimination

Yet this apparent good news comes as bad news to those born with genetic susceptibilities to disease, because medical care is funded by private insurance companies and medical insurance is tied to employment. An identifiable genetic predisposition to disease counts as an existing condition, and insurance companies are beginning to deny coverage to people with existing conditions. As new techniques for prevention and therapy become available, the very people who could benefit may be denied access to them.

Paul Billings, a genetics researcher and ethicist at Stanford University Medical School, has collected anecdotal evidence of genetic discrimination. Testifying before Congress, Billings told of a woman who, during a routine physical, spoke to her physician about the possibility of her mother having Huntington's disease. Later, when the woman applied for life insurance, her medical records were reviewed and she lost all her insurance.

In another case, a 14-month-old girl was diagnosed with phenylketonuria through a newborn screening program. A low phenylalanine diet was prescribed, and her parents followed the diet rules. The child has grown up to be a normal and healthy person. Her health care at birth was covered by a group insurance policy associated with her father's employment, but when he changed jobs the new carrier declared her ineligible for coverage. Once a genetic predisposition for an expensive disease becomes part of one's medical record, insurance carriers and employers connected to them find it in their best financial interest to minimize or deny health coverage.

In a report by the Committee on Government Operations, U.S. Representative John Conyers (D., Michigan) responded to Billings and others:

> "Like discrimination based on race, genetic discrimination is wrong because it is based on hereditary characteristics we are powerless to change. The fear in the minds of many people is that genetic information will be used to identify those with 'weak' or 'inferior' genes, who will then be treated as a 'biological underclass.'". . .

Prenatal Genetic Testing and Selective Abortion

Can we forecast a connection between genetic discrimination and selective abortion [selectively aborting some fetuses and not others based on their genetic makeup]? Yes. A couple in Louisiana had a child with cystic fibrosis, a genetic disorder leading to chronic lung infections and excruciating discomfort. When the wife became pregnant with the second child, a prenatal genetic test revealed that the fetus carried the mutant gene for cystic fibrosis. The couple's health maintenance organization demanded that they abort. If they refused to abort, the HMO would withdraw coverage from both the newborn and the first child. Only when the couple threatened to sue did the HMO back down and grant coverage for the second child.

With the advance of prenatal genetic testing, both parents and insurance carriers can find out whether a child may be prone to having a debilitating and expensive disease. It is not unrealistic to imagine the insurance industry publishing a list of disqualifying genetic predispositions. If one of the predispositions were found in a fetus, the industry would mandate an abortion under penalty of loss of coverage. This would outrage pro-life parents, and even pro-choice parents would find this financial pressure to be the equivalent of a compromise on choice.

We are moving step-by-step toward this selective abortion scenario. In addition to feeling pressure from the privately funded insurance industry, parents themselves will likely develop criteria for deciding which fetuses will be brought to term and which will be aborted. Genetic criteria will play a major role. Prenatal testing to identify disease-related genes will become routine, and tests for hundreds of deleterious genes may become part of the prenatal arsenal. Parents wanting what they believe to be a perfectly healthy child may abort repeatedly at each hint of a genetic disorder. Choice and selection will enter the enterprise of baby making at a magnitude unimaginable in previous history.

Most families will confront the issue when they find themselves in a clinic office talking with a genetic counselor. Although a genetic analysis of heritable family traits can help immensely in planning for future children, talking with a genetic counselor too often begins when a pregnancy is already in progress. The task of the genetic counselor is to provide information regarding the degree of risk that a given child might be born with a genetic disorder, and to impart this information objectively, impartially and confidentially (when possible) so that the autonomy of the parents is protected.

A Difficult Choice

What is surprising and disconcerting to mothers or couples in this situation is that genetic risk is usually given statistically, in percentages. The parents find themselves with difficult-to-interpret information while facing an unknown future. Conflicting values between marital partners or even within each of them increase the difficulty—and the anxiety.

Both genetic endowment and degree of disability are relative unknowns. For a recessive defective gene such as that for cystic fibrosis, when both parents are carriers the risk is 50 percent that the child will also be a carrier and 25 percent that the child will contract the disease. With this information, parents decide to proceed toward birth or to terminate the pregnancy. Later in the pregnancy the specific genetic makeup of a fetus can be discerned via amniocentesis and other tests.

In cases of Down Syndrome, for example, which is associated with trisomy (three copies of chromosome 21), eight out of every ten negative prenatal diagnoses lead to the decision to abort. Even though the genetic predisposition can be clearly identified in this way, the degree of mental retardation that will result is unknown. Mild cases mean near-average intelligence. Yet the choice to abort has become the virtual norm. The population of Down Syndrome people in our society is dropping, making this a form of eugenics by popular choice.

Joel Pett for the *Lexington Herald-Leader*. Reprinted with permission.

In only 3 to 5 percent of cases does a positive prenatal diagnosis reveal the presence of a genetic disorder so severe that the probable level of suffering on the part of the child warrants that a parent consider abortion. In making this judgment, I am invoking a principle of compassion—what bioethicists dub the principle of nonmaleficence, or reducing human suffering whenever possible. In situations where such a diagnosis is made and where prospective parents strongly desire to bring a child into the world, a number of things happen.

First, genetic counselors report that parents automatically refer to the child as a "baby," never as a "fetus." They clearly think of the life growing in the womb as a person. Second, when confronted with the bad news, they experience turmoil.

The turmoil usually leads to a decision to terminate the pregnancy, but not always. It is not the job of the genetic counselor to encourage abortion; even advocates of choice on abortion defend the parents' right to decide to bring such a child to birth. Third, even when the decision to terminate is made, the grieving parents see their decision as an expression of their love, not a denial of love. It is an act of compassion.

The Perfect-Child Syndrome

The distinction between convenience and compassion is ethically significant here. As the practice of prenatal genetic testing expands and the principle of autonomy—the responsibility for choice—is applied to the parents and not to the unborn child, the total number of abortions will increase, perhaps dramatically. Each pregnancy will be thought of as tentative until the fetus has passed dozens or hundreds of genetic tests. A culturally reinforced image of the desirable child—the perfect-child syndrome—may lead couples to try repeated pregnancies, terminating the undesirables and giving birth only to the "best" test passers. Those born in this fashion risk being commodified by their parents. In addition, those who might be born with a disability and with the potential for leading a productive and fulfilling life might never see the light of day.

A social byproduct of selective abortion might be increased discrimination against people living with disabilities. The assumption could grow that to live with a disability is to have a life not worth living. Persons with disabilities fear that the medical establishment and its supportive social policies will seek to prevent "future people like me" from ever being born. The inference is: "I am worthless to society." The imputation of dignity to handicapped persons may be quietly withdrawn as they are increasingly viewed as unnecessary and expensive appendages to an otherwise healthy society.

This would be a tragedy of the first order. Disabled persons deserve dignity and encouragement. Such people frequently gain victory in their difficult life struggles. Most disabled people report that while the disability, the pain, and the need for compensatory devices and assistance can produce considerable inconvenience, the inconveniences become minimal or even forgotten once individuals make the transition to living their everyday lives.

Whether we like it or not, the advancing frontier of genetics, with its impact on reproductive technology, thrusts us back into the abortion debate. *Roe v. Wade* (1973) did not answer the questions we will be asking in 2003. The Supreme Court decided that a woman has the right to abort during the first trimester. Genetic discrimination raises an additional question: by what criteria might a fetus be considered abortable? *Roe v. Wade* focuses on the woman's right to decide what to do with her body; now we focus on the fetuses and the criteria by which some will live and others will not. A skeptic might say that as long as the woman has the right to choose, it is a moot point to talk of criteria of choice. I believe that while a woman's right to choose is a legal matter, the criteria for choosing are an ethical matter.

Even though abortion on request is legal, not all grounds for requesting it are ethical. In the case of selective abortion, a decision based solely on the desires of the parents without regard for the child's well-being is unethical. As Martin Luther said, "Even if a child is unattractive when it is born, we nevertheless love it."

Five Axioms to Guide Christians in the Era of Selective Abortion

Most Christians are not ethically ready for the era of selective abortion. We are unprepared for the kind of decisions that large numbers of prospective parents will be confronting. We have thought about the issue of abortion on request and the question of when human dignity begins, but now we need middle axioms to guide the choices that will confront the next generation of parents.

First, we need to identify defective or undesirable genes prior to conception rather than after. Whether or not the conceptus has full personhood and full dignity comparable to living adults, ethicists agree that the fertilized zygote deserves a level of respect and honor that resists brute manipulation or irreverent discarding. Genetic selection in the sperm or ovum prior to fertilization, prior to the DNA blueprint of a potential person, seems more defensible.

Second, the choice for selective abortion should be the last resort. Prefertilization selection should be given priority when possible, as should prenatal gene therapy.

Third, the motive of compassion that seeks to minimize suffering on the part of children coming into the world should hold relative sway when choosing for or against selective abortion. Compassion, taken up as the principle of nonmaleficence in bioethics, constitutes the way that parents show love toward children-to-be. In rare cases (3 to 5 percent of prenatal diagnoses), the genetic disorder is so severe that no approximation to a fulfilling life is possible. The decision to abort can be understood as a form of caring for the baby as well as self-care for the parents. Yet it is still a judgment call. No clear rule tells us exactly when the imputed dignity of the unborn child may be trumped by a compassionate decision to abort.

Fourth, we should distinguish between acts of eugenics and acts of compassion. The goal of eugenics is to reduce the incidence of a certain genetic trait, usually an undesirable trait. Eugenics is social in scope and derives from some social philosophy. At this point, bioethicists tend to oppose eugenic policies because, if practiced on a large scale, they could reduce biodiversity. More important, eugenics connotes the political totalitarianism of the Third Reich. The compassion or nonmaleficence principle, when limited to the concrete situation of a family making a decision regarding a particular child, is much more acceptable. The line between eugenics and compassion is not a clear one, however. Some will argue that the attempt to eliminate a recessive gene for something like cystic fibrosis in future branches on a family tree is an act of compassion.

Fifth, we should distinguish between preventing suffering and enhancing genetic potential. Genetic selection to help reduce suffering is an act that, in at least a minimal sense, is directed toward the well-being of the child. In the future, when genetic selection and perhaps even genetic engineering make possible designer babies with higher-than-average intelligence, good looks or athletic prowess, then we will move closer to embracing the perfect-child syndrome. The risk of commodifying children and evaluating them according to standards of quality control increases when parents are "buying." The risk of commodification does not in itself constitute a reason to reject all genetic therapy, but it does call us to bolster a sound, biblically defensible principle: God loves people regardless of their genetic makeup, and we should do likewise.

"What matters morally is preventing avoidable pain and suffering that actual people will have to experience."

Genetic Screening Can Be Ethical

Walter Glannon

Walter Glannon, a professor of philosophy at the University of Calgary, argues in the following viewpoint that it is ethically acceptable to use genetic screening to prevent the birth of people with genetic diseases. He acknowledges that the selective abortion of fetuses with genetic abnormalities would be morally objectionable to many, and argues that genetic screening is most ethically acceptable when it is applied to embryos that have been created in vitro—so-called "test-tube babies." Glannon concludes that using genetic screening to prevent the existence of people with severe disabilities is an ethically justifiable form of eugenics, since it prevents the suffering those people would endure.

As you read, consider the following questions:
1. What two principles does the author use to justify the selective termination of embryos with genetic disease?
2. In Glannon's opinion, why is preimplantation of embryos slated for in vitro fertilization preferable to amniocentesis of fetuses in the womb?
3. How does the author describe "utopian genetics"?

Excerpted from Walter Glannon, "Genes, Embryos, and Future People," *Bioethics*, July 1998. Reprinted with permission from Blackwell Publishers.

There are three basic types of genetic alteration. Gene therapy consists in the correction or addition of genes in the somatic (body) cells of a person to treat a disease the person already has, where the aim of treatment is to cure the disease or alleviate its symptoms. By contrast, genetic alteration of germ cells (gametes; sperm and egg) at the zygotic or embryonic stage of the human organism prevents diseased persons from coming into existence. . . . Genetic enhancement involves non-therapeutic alteration of genes aimed at improving cognitive and physical functioning which already are at or above the normal level for persons.

The three types of genetic alteration which I have mentioned are to be distinguished further from selective termination of embryos after genetic testing has revealed the presence of disease-causing genes, or markers for these genes, in the cells of embryos. Germ-line genetic testing and termination is not a therapeutic but a preventive strategy designed to avoid the existence of individuals who would be severely disabled and have restricted lives. . . .

Only Embryos with Severe Genetic Defects Should Be Terminated

Present biotechnology allows us to test embryonic cells for genetic abnormalities that lead directly to severe early-onset disorders, like Tay-Sachs disease, Hurler syndrome, Lesch-Nyhan syndrome, and Canavan's disease, as well as late-onset disorders like Huntington's disease. We also can test embryos for genes that predispose people to chronic and ultimately fatal conditions like coronary heart disease and cancer. Genetic mutations play a causal role in many diseases by altering a crucial enzyme or other protein. The alteration may occur in differing degrees, depending on the extent of interaction between genes and the environment. In the specific diseases I mentioned above, though, environment plays little or no causal role in their occurrence. Either the defective gene necessarily causes the disease, or else it has a very high probability of causing it (95% with the Huntington's gene).

In Tay-Sachs, for instance, babies appear quite normal at birth. But in the first year of life their nervous systems degenerate, and they usually die by the time they reach 3 or 4.

This disease is caused by the presence of two copies of an abnormal gene, or mutant allele, at a particular site on one of the 23 chromosome pairs. Tay-Sachs is an autosomal recessive disorder, which effectively means that the child inherits one mutant allele from each parent. Through the fusion of the gametes in the zygote that develops into the embryo, fetus, and person, the parents transmit the disease to their child.

Ideally, we would use gene therapy by inserting an additional normal copy of the defective gene into the relevant cells and thus cure the disease. But Tay-Sachs, like most recessive (and dominant) disorders, has not proven amenable to therapy. Alternatively, we can test and selectively terminate embryos with genes that cause this or other severely disabling diseases, preventing these diseases by preventing the existence of the people who would have them. This practice can be justified on two grounds. Beneficence requires that we not harm people by causing them to experience pain and suffering over the balance of their lives. In addition, justice requires that we not deny severely disabled people the same opportunities for achieving a good life as are open to others who are healthy or have only moderate cognitive or physical disabilities. Arguably, the justice requirement will apply to only a small number of people, since the idea of equal opportunity for a good life implies a certain number of years to undertake and complete projects for a decent minimum level of well-being, and most people with severe early-onset genetically caused diseases have relatively short lifespans. Perhaps this is not the case with a disease like CF [cystic fibrosis], where people afflicted often live for 30 years or more. But I do not believe that this genetically caused disease is so severely disabling and painful that we can justifiably prevent the lives of the persons who would have it. Considerations of justice matter; but what matters more than ensuring equal opportunity for achieving a good life is preventing avoidable severe pain and suffering that people actually experience once they exist. These are what make lives not worth living on the whole. Indeed, it is often the severe pain and suffering associated with disabilities which preclude people from having the opportunities to achieve a decent minimum level of lifetime well-being.

Preventing Pain and Suffering

Testing of embryonic cells for genetic abnormalities may be done by extracting cells from preimplantation IVF [in vitro fertilization] embryos. To produce extracorporeal IVF embryos for this type of testing, fertility drugs such as Clomid or Pergonal can be given to a woman to induce superovulation and in turn produce a number of eggs that can be recovered for fertilization with sperm. One advantage of producing multiple embryos is that, if genetic abnormalities are detected in any one of the embryos, then it can be selectively terminated and another, normal, embryo can be implanted in the woman's uterus. This would enable parents to have a normal child instead of a disabled one and to avoid any burdens that such a child might have on them or, if they have other children, the rest of the family. . . .

Parents Can Genetically Harm Their Children

When a child is born and grows, the child and others inevitably measure its life in terms of the other lives it might reasonably be thought to have lived in its family and time. . . . It is by no means senseless for a person to think "If my mother had only waited a few months until after the rubella epidemic had passed to conceive me, 'I' would never [have] been born with this deformity." Taken strictly, this statement is nonsense: the child who could have been conceived and born after a delay of some months is not the same child as the one who was conceived and born earlier. But if we think of ourselves before conception or birth as an imaginary fungible intended child of our parents, who could come into being with roughly the same physical and mental attributes as other children, this statement makes perfect sense. Because parents are properly regarded as proxy decision-makers for their child's health status, it is therefore reasonable for a child to feel wronged when poor decision making by parents (or by those who advise them) leads the child to be born with serious impairments or suffering relative to others in its birth cohort.

Ronald M. Green, *Journal of Law, Medicine, and Ethics*, Spring 1997.

Another attractive feature of this method, as Robert Edwards explains, is that

Identifying embryos with genetic abnormalities would offer

an alternative to amniocentesis during the second trimester of pregnancy, and the "abortion" *in vitro* of a defective preimplantation embryo . . . would be infinitely preferable to abortion *in vivo* at twenty weeks of pregnancy or thereabouts as the results of amniocentesis are obtained.

Testing preimplantation IVF embryos for genetic abnormalities would be preferable to testing fetal cells for these abnormalities by amniocentesis or chorionic villus sampling because, unlike these invasive procedures, it would not be painful to the pregnant woman and would avoid certain medical risks. Specifically, putting a needle into the uterus to extract cells from either the amniotic fluid or embryonic membrane triggers a miscarriage once in every 50 to 100 pregnancies. Moreover, villus sampling may cause limb deformities in the fetus.

Terminating the development of one embryo and implanting a different embryo would mean that the life of one potential person was not allowed to become actual and that the life of a different potential person became actual instead. The same number of people would exist, but they would be different people. Yet whether one or a different potential person is allowed to exist does not matter morally. Rather, what matters morally is preventing avoidable pain and suffering that actual people will have to experience. And to the extent that an embryo containing a disease-causing gene will result in severe pain and suffering in the person who develops from it, we are morally required to prevent the disease, pain, and suffering by terminating the development of that embryo. What must be emphasized, however, is that the moral requirement to terminate embryos and thereby prevent certain people from coming into existence pertains only to those people who would have *severe*, not just moderately severe, diseases. Only severe diseases make people's lives not worth living on the whole. . . .

Objections from Disabilities Rights Advocates

Two objections might be raised against the claim that people with severe disease or disability should not be brought into existence. Disabilities rights advocates might argue that intervention in the form of testing and selectively terminating genetically defective embryos would reduce the number of people with disabilities. Consequently, public support for persons who already have disabilities would erode. It would lead to a devaluation of the lives of the disabled and to discrimination against them. To rebut this objection, we can appeal to Allen Buchanan's point that 'it is not the *people* with disabilities which we devalue, it is the *disabilities*'. Buchanan further says 'we devalue disabilities because we value the opportunities and welfare of the people who have them—and it is because we value people, all people, that we care about limitations on their welfare and opportunities. We also know that disabilities, as such, diminish opportunities and welfare, even when they are *not so severe* that the lives of those who have them are not worth living'. The underlying rationale for this position is that it is a matter of justice, not only beneficence, that we remove or prevent limitations on an individual's opportunities for a decent life. But the second passage cited from Buchanan leaves open the possibility that it is morally permissible to terminate embryos with genetic defects that would lead to people having lives with limited opportunities that are nonetheless worth living. Against Buchanan, I believe that we should terminate only those embryos with genetic defects that manifest themselves in severe disabilities that make life on balance not worth living. . . .

Utopian Genetics

A second objection to my view is that any form of genetic intervention is motivated by the desire to improve the human species through selection. This amounts to a program of positive eugenics, which would lead to a repeat of the inhumane treatment of people and a violation of their intrinsic worth which have occurred in recent history. To this objection, we can respond by saying that the aim of any medically and morally defensible form of genetic intervention should not be to enhance people's genotype or phenotypic traits, but only to ensure that the people we do cause to exist have normal, or close to normal, cognitive and physical functioning over the balance of their lives. In preventing the existence of people with severe disability, we are not aiming to enhance or improve lives that already are, or would be, at a decent minimum level of well-being, but only to ensure that the people we do bring into existence will not fall well below this level. . . . We have no moral duty to bring people into existence with good lives. But if we do bring people into existence, we have a moral duty to ensure that their lives do not contain so much pain and suffering as to be not worth living for them on the whole.

The negative eugenics I am defending has affinities with what Philip Kitcher calls 'utopian eugenics'. This involves a policy guaranteeing that people have reproductive freedom in choosing which embryos they allow to develop and subsequently the people they bring into existence. Their choices must be free of any socially coercive pressure to prevent people from existing for economic reasons or perfectionist ideals. Provided that genetic testing and selective termination of defective embryos are practiced in order to prevent extreme pain and suffering in people, not to enhance their cognitive and physical capacities above the normal range, and that reproductive technologies like IVF and genetic testing are affordable and accessible to all, utopian eugenics is a morally justifiable policy.

"Real human clones will simply be later-born identical twins—nothing more and nothing less."

Human Cloning Is Ethical

Lee M. Silver

Lee M. Silver is a molecular biologist and the author of *Remaking Eden: Cloning and Beyond in a Brave New World*. In the following viewpoint, he describes the shock and moral outrage many people have expressed regarding the prospect of human cloning. Silver believes these sentiments are misguided. He rejects three arguments against cloning: the notion that the cloning will produce genetic defects in the cloned individuals; the fear that human clones will wish they were not clones; and the argument that cloning will somehow disrupt the process of evolution. Silver concludes that most people oppose human cloning on religious grounds, which he feels are insufficient to shape public policy on human cloning.

As you read, consider the following questions:
1. What rationale did the National Bioethics Advisory Board use to justify its proposal to ban human cloning in the United States, according to the author?
2. What is Daniel Callahan's argument against human cloning, as quoted by Silver, and how does Silver respond to it?
3. What response does Silver offer to the idea that human cloning is equivalent to playing God?

Reprinted from Lee M. Silver, "Cloning, Ethics, and Beyond," *Cambridge Quarterly of Healthcare Ethics*, Spring 1998. Reprinted with permission from Cambridge University Press.

On Sunday morning, 23 February 1997, the world awoke to a technological advance that shook the foundations of biology and philosophy. On that day, we were introduced to Dolly, a 6-month-old lamb that had been cloned directly from a single cell taken from the breast tissue of an adult donor. Perhaps more astonished by this accomplishment than any of their neighbors were the scientists who actually worked in the field of mammalian genetics and embryology. Outside the lab where the cloning had actually taken place, most of us thought it could never happen. Oh, we would say that perhaps at some point in the distant future, cloning might become feasible through the use of sophisticated biotechnologies far beyond those available to us now. But what many of us really believed, deep in our hearts, was that this was one biological feat we could never master. New life—in the special sense of a conscious being—must have its origins in an embryo formed through the merger of gametes from a mother and father. It was impossible, we thought, for a cell from an adult mammal to become reprogrammed, to start all over again, to generate another entire animal or person in the image of the one born earlier.

How wrong we were.

Scientists Will Soon Be Able to Clone Humans

Of course, it wasn't the cloning of a sheep that stirred the imaginations of hundreds of millions of people. It was the idea that humans could now be cloned as well, and many people were terrified by the prospect. Ninety percent of Americans polled within the first week after the story broke felt that human cloning should be banned. And while not unanimous, the opinions of many media pundits, ethicists, and policymakers seemed to follow that of the public at large. The idea that humans might be cloned was called "morally despicable," "repugnant," "totally inappropriate," as well as "ethically wrong, socially misguided and biologically mistaken."

Scientists who work directly in the field of animal genetics and embryology were dismayed by all the attention that now bore down on their research. Most unhappy of all were those associated with the biotechnology industry, which has the most to gain in the short-term from animal applications of the cloning technology. Their fears were not unfounded. In the aftermath of Dolly, polls found that two out of three Americans considered the cloning of *animals* to be morally unacceptable, while 56% said they would not eat meat from cloned animals.

It should not be surprising, then, that scientists tried to play down the feasibility of human cloning. First they said that it might not be possible *at all* to transfer the technology to human cells. And even if human cloning is possible in theory, they said, "it would take years of trial and error before it could be applied successfully," so that "cloning in humans is unlikely any time soon." And even if it becomes possible to apply the technology successfully, they said, "there is no clinical reason why you would do this." And even if a person wanted to clone him- or herself or someone else, he or she wouldn't be able to find trained medical professionals who would be willing to do it.

Really? That's not what science, history, or human nature suggest to me. The cloning of Dolly broke the technological barrier. There is no reason to expect that the technology couldn't be transferred to human cells. On the contrary, there is every reason to expect that it *can* be transferred. If nuclear transplantation works in every mammalian species in which it has been seriously tried, then nuclear transplantation *will* work with human cells as well. It requires only equipment and facilities that are already standard, or easy to obtain by biomedical laboratories and freestanding in vitro fertilization clinics across the world. Although the protocol itself demands the services of highly trained and skilled personnel, there are thousands of people with such skills in dozens of countries.

Misconceptions About Cloning

The initial horror elicited by the announcement of Dolly's birth was due in large part to a misunderstanding by the lay public and the media of what biological cloning is and is not. The science critic Jeremy Rifkin exclaimed: "It's a horrendous crime to make a Xerox (copy) of someone," and the Irvine, California, rabbi Bernard King was seriously frightened when he asked, "Can the cloning create a soul? Can scientists create the soul that would make a being ethical, moral, caring, loving, all the things we attribute humanity to?" The Catholic priest Father Saunders suggested that "cloning would only produce humanoids or androids—soulless replicas of human beings that could be used as slaves." And *New York Times* writer Brent Staples warned us that "synthetic humans would be easy prey for humanity's worst instincts."

Real human clones will simply be later-born identical twins—nothing more and nothing less. Cloned children will be full-fledged human beings, indistinguishable in biological terms from all other members of the species. But even with this understanding, many ethicists, scholars, and scientists are still vehemently opposed to the use of cloning as means of human reproduction under any circumstances whatsoever. Why do they feel this way? Why does this new reproductive technology upset them so?

First, they say, it's a question of "safety." The cloning procedure has not been proven safe and, as a result, its application toward the generation of newborn children could produce deformities and other types of birth defects. Second, they say that even if physical defects can be avoided, there is the psychological well-being of the cloned child to consider. And third, above and beyond each individual child, they are worried about the horrible effect that cloning will have on society as a whole.

What I will argue here is that people who voice any one or more of these concerns are—either consciously or subconsciously—hiding the real reason they oppose cloning. They have latched on to arguments about safety, psychology, and society because they are simply unable to come up with an ethical argument that is not based on the religious notion that by cloning human beings man will be playing God, and it is wrong to play God.

Human Cloning Will Not Lead to Genetic Defects

Let us take a look at the safety argument first. Throughout the 20th century, medical scientists have sought to develop new protocols and drugs for treating disease and alleviating human suffering. The safety of all these new medical proto-

Arguments Against Cloning and Their Responses

Argument: Cloning is an affront to human dignity.

Response: Usually people who make this argument are unable to explain why cloning offends human dignity. The argument is supposed to be self-evident. The argument is based on "genetic essentialism," or "genetic determinism" a belief that one's unique humanness is entirely a product of one's DNA. The argument is reductionist and itself an affront to human dignity. . . .

Argument: Cloning is unnatural.

Response: Nature creates clones all the time, as identical twins. . . .

Argument: It's all right if nature makes clones, but if we do it we're "playing God."

Response: Modern medicine rarely leaves matters to "Nature." We use IVF [in vitro fertilization], try to keep 700-gram newborns alive, and, where culture and religion permit, use donor sperm, eggs, or embryos. Why is cloning different from other reproductive technologies? . . .

Argument: Clones will be treated as second-rate, because they're "carbon copies." Isn't this an affront to dignity?

Response: This is a "science fiction" view. Do twins feel "second rate" because each looks like the other? . . .

Argument: Wealthy people will clone themselves to have organ banks of "spare parts" in case they need hearts or livers. These clones could be made without heads, so they could be killed for organs without committing murder.

Response: Using another person for "spare parts" is murder and would be prosecuted as such. Clones are undeniably persons. Making "headless clones" to supply organs would also be murder. It would require decerebrating (removing the higher brain) of a fetus or infant. Since the fetus or infant falls under the same legal/ethical rules as a non-cloned fetus or infant, whoever did this would be prosecuted. Furthermore, there is no need to create an entire human. Individual tissues or organs could be grown.

Dorothy C. Wertz, *The Gene Letter*, August 1998.

---

cols was initially unknown. But through experimental testing on animals first, and then volunteer human subjects, safety could be ascertained and governmental agencies—such as the Food and Drug Administration in the United States—could make a decision as to whether the new protocol or drug should be approved for use in standard medical practice.

It would be ludicrous to suggest that legislatures should pass laws banning the application of each newly imagined medical protocol before its safety has been determined. Professional ethics committees, institutional review boards, and the individual ethics of each medical practitioner are relied upon to make sure that hundreds of new experimental protocols are tested and used in an appropriate manner each year. And yet the question of unknown safety alone was the single rationale used by the National Bioethics Advisory Board (NBAC) to propose a ban on human cloning in the United States.

Opposition to cloning on the basis of safety alone is almost surely a losing proposition. Although the media have concocted fantasies of dozens of malformed monster lambs paving the way for the birth of Dolly, fantasy is all it was. Of the 277 fused cells created by Wilmut and his colleagues, only 29 developed into embryos. These 29 embryos were placed into 13 ewes, of which 1 became pregnant and gave birth to Dolly. If safety is measured by the percentage of lambs born in good health, then the record, so far, is 100% for nuclear transplantation from an adult cell (albeit with a sample size of 1).

In fact, there is no scientific basis for the belief that cloned children will be any more prone to genetic problems than naturally conceived children. The commonest type of birth defect results from the presence of an abnormal number of chromosomes in the fertilized egg. This birth defect arises during gamete production and, as such, its frequency should be greatly reduced in embryos formed by cloning. The second most common class of birth defects results from the inheritance of two mutant copies of a gene from two parents who are silent carriers. With cloning, any silent mutation in a donor will be silent in the newly formed embryo and child as well. Finally, much less frequently, birth defects can be caused by new mutations; these will occur with the same frequency in embryos derived through conception or cloning. (Although some scientists have suggested that chromosome shortening in the donor cell will cause cloned children to have a shorter lifespan, there is every reason to expect that chromosome repair in the embryo will eliminate this problem.) Surprisingly, what our current scientific understanding suggests is that birth defects in cloned children could occur less frequently than birth defects in naturally conceived ones.

Human Cloning Will Not Harm the Cloned Child

Once safety has been eliminated as an objection to cloning, the next concern voiced is the psychological well-being of the child. Daniel Callahan, the former director of the Hastings Center, argues that "engineering someone's entire genetic makeup would compromise his or her right to a unique identity." But no such 'right' has been granted by nature—identical twins are born every day as natural clones of each other. Dr. Callahan would have to concede this fact, but he might still argue that just because twins occur naturally does not mean we should create them on purpose.

Dr. Callahan might argue that a cloned child is harmed by knowledge of her future condition. He might say that it's unfair to go through childhood knowing what you will look like as an adult, or being forced to consider future medical ailments that might befall you. But even in the absence of cloning, many children have some sense of the future possibilities encoded in the genes they got from their parents. Furthermore, genetic screening already provides people with the ability to learn about hundreds of disease predispositions. And as genetic knowledge and technology become more and more sophisticated, it will become possible for any human being to learn even more about his or her genetic future than a cloned child could learn from his or her progenitor's past.

It might also be argued that a cloned child will be harmed by having to live up to unrealistic expectations placed on her by her parents. But there is no reason to believe that her parents will be any more unreasonable than many other parents who expect their children to accomplish in their lives what they were unable to accomplish in their own. No one would argue that parents with such tendencies should be prohibited from having children.

But let's grant that among the many cloned children brought into this world, some *will* feel badly about the fact that their genetic constitution is not unique. Is this alone a strong enough reason to ban the practice of cloning? Before answering this question, ask yourself another: Is a child having knowledge of an older twin worse off than a child born into poverty? If we ban the former, shouldn't we ban the latter? Why is it that so many politicians seem to care so much about cloning but so little about the welfare of children in general?

Human Cloning Will Not Harm Society

Finally, there are those who argue against cloning based on the perception that it will harm society at large in some way. The *New York Times* columnist William Safire expresses the opinion of many others when he says that "cloning's identicality would restrict evolution." This is bad, he argues, because "the continued interplay of genes . . . is central to humankind's progress." But Mr. Safire is wrong on both practical and theoretical grounds. On practical grounds, even if human cloning became efficient, legal, and popular among those in the moneyed classes (which is itself highly unlikely), it would still only account for a fraction of a percent of all the children born onto this earth. Furthermore, each of the children born by cloning to different families would be different from each other, so where does the identicality come from?

On theoretical grounds, Safire is wrong because humankind's progress has nothing to do with unfettered evolution, which is always unpredictable and not necessarily upward bound. H.G. Wells recognized this principle in his 1895 novel *The Time Machine*, which portrays the evolution of humankind into weak and dimwitted but cuddly little creatures. And Kurt Vonnegut follows this same theme in *Galápagos*, where he suggests that our "big brains" will be the cause of our downfall, and future humans with smaller brains and powerful flippers will be the only remnants of a once great species, a million years hence.

Only Religious Objections to Human Cloning Remain

As is so often the case with new reproductive technologies, the real reason that people condemn cloning has nothing to do with technical feasibility, child psychology, societal well-being, or the preservation of the human species. The real reason derives from religious beliefs. It is the sense that cloning leaves God out of the process of human creation, and that man is venturing into places he does not belong. Of course, the 'playing God' objection only makes sense in the context of one definition of God, as a supernatural being who plays a role in the birth of each new member of our species. And even if one holds this particular view of God, it does not necessarily follow that cloning is equivalent to playing God. Some who consider themselves to be religious have argued that if God didn't want man to clone, "he" wouldn't have made it possible.

Should public policy in a pluralist society be based on a narrow religious point of view? Most people would say no, which is why those who hold this point of view are grasping for secular reasons to support their call for an unconditional ban on the cloning of human beings. When the dust clears from the cloning debate, however, the secular reasons will almost certainly have disappeared. And then, only religious objections will remain.

> *"Cloning would take the humanity out of human reproduction, and in doing so rob our spirits of something that cannot be replaced artificially."*

Human Cloning Is Unethical

E.V. Kontorovich

In the following viewpoint, E.V. Kontorovich defends his belief that human cloning is morally repugnant. Cloning is inhumane, he contends, and there are no good reasons why it should be performed on humans. The proposed medical uses for human cloning are in fact unethical, he writes, as they include the harvesting of organs from cloned human fetuses. Cloning as a means of overcoming infertility is little better, in Kontorovich's view: The relationship between the parent and his or her cloned child would be very ambiguous, and the clone might be viewed as a commodity that was made rather than a person who was born. Kontorovich is a writer living in New York.

As you read, consider the following questions:

1. After the news of Dolly the cloned sheep broke in 1997, what percentage of Americans found human cloning morally repugnant, according to Kontorovich?
2. According to the author, what is the most likely way in which cloning would be used to help alleviate illness?
3. In Kontorovich's opinion, in what ways is human cloning like incest?

Reprinted from E.V. Kontorovich, "Asexual Revolution," *National Review*, March 9, 1998. Copyright ©1998 National Review, Inc., 215 Lexington Avenue, New York, NY 10016. Reprinted with permission from National Review, Inc.

[In 1997], an obscure Scottish veterinarian named Ian Wilmut demonstrated how to make mammals, and by implication humans, in a laboratory without any act of sexual congress, indeed without sperm or an (intact) egg. Through cloning, a near-perfect genetic replica of a person could be grown from a single cell of skin, or, say, of rib. In the years since, cloning technology has developed rapidly. Experiments on cattle have refined the technique, and chimpanzee embryos have been successfully cloned. The possibility of human cloning now looms imminently, unseen but real.

The Almost Unanimous Outcry Against Human Cloning

When the cloned sheep, Dolly, first hit the newspapers, nearly 90 per cent of Americans found human cloning morally repugnant, according to every poll. Perhaps no other moral issue in American history has produced such near unanimity—not slavery, not Prohibition, not abortion. But politicians have been reluctant to cement this consensus into federal law.

A bill introduced in the Senate by Christopher Bond (R., Missouri) would have outlawed human cloning under a penalty of up to ten years in prison. It lost under a hail of criticism from medical groups, and even some conservative Republicans, that it would be an unnecessary impediment to scientific research. This is a seductive argument, especially when cancer victims like Senator Connie Mack (R., Florida) make it.

But the talk of concrete material benefits from cloning assumes that if it is permissible to reproduce certain cells for certain purposes (e.g., to reproduce a burn victim's remaining healthy skin cells to produce a graft), it is permissible to reproduce human beings in a petri dish.

Humans are embodied beings, our souls and physical selves are profoundly intertwined. Cloning would take the humanity out of human reproduction, and in so doing rob our spirits of something that cannot be replaced artificially. Furthermore, the manufacture of human beings on demand without conception would turn people into made-to-order goods, and would in aggregate debase our respect for human life.

Most advocates of cloning ignore the moral arguments

and tempt us with small concrete benefits. These potential benefits—many of which, such as a cure for cancer, seem sheer fantasy—play on our current notions of rights and our culture of compassion in a way that gives them considerable political force. But these arguments constitute an end-run around the central issues. They do not sustain scrutiny.

The Advocates of Human Cloning

There is little disagreement about the profound effects the cloning of human beings would have on human nature. However, some cloning apologists simply respond, "So what?" For example, Harvard Law professor Laurence Tribe sees flaws in "a society that bans acts of human creation for no better reason than that their particular form defies nature and tradition." Princeton molecular biologist Lee Silver makes a stronger case than many critics do, that cloning would completely redefine human life, but embraces this outcome as a way for us to take control of our destiny as a species and reshape it as we see fit.

We hear most often that cloning could provide perfectly compatible body parts for persons who need them or that it could enable infertile couples and homosexuals to have "biological" offspring. It it hard to say without sounding callous, but death and bodily infirmity are concomitant with human existence and in the long run unavoidable. We live in a society where longevity is becoming a value in itself, but longevity cannot justify a practice that is basically wrong.

As for infertility, it is not even a disabling sickness that, on humanitarian grounds, we should feel obliged to alleviate. It is simply a limitation, on the order of not being tall or wealthy. There is nothing heartless about saying that people should resort to alternatives besides cloning, like adoption. As for those whose arguments are informed by the belief that people have a right to make use of whatever new technologies become available, even Laurence Tribe concedes that there can be no such general right.

The Prospect of Human Organ Farms

When defenders of cloning talk about the brave new world of medical techniques they skip over the fact that its most wondrous manufactures would be Calibans. Consider the likeliest way in which cloning can be used to help with illness: through the creation of perfectly compatible organs for transplantation. It is important here to remember what cloning entails: the DNA-laden nucleus from a somatic (body) cell is placed into a denucleated egg and stimulated into growth with an electric shock. What begins to grow is a "fertilized" egg, an embryo—not a kidney or any other disembodied piece of tissue.

The Ends Do Not Justify the Means

"Cloning human beings is unethical and dehumanizing, you say? Never mind: it will help us treat infertility, avoid genetic disease, and provide perfect materials for organ replacement." Such, indeed, was the tenor of the June 1997 report of the National Bioethics Advisory Commission on Cloning Human Beings. Notwithstanding its call for a temporary ban on the practice, the only moral objection the commission could agree upon was that cloning "is not safe to use in humans at this time" because the technique has yet to be perfected. Even this elite ethical body, in other words, was unable to muster any other moral argument sufficient to cause us to forgo the possible health benefits of cloning.

The same argument will inevitably also justify creating and growing human embryos for experimentation, revising the definition of death to facilitate organ transplantation, growing human body parts in the peritoneal cavities of animals, perfusing newly dead bodies as factories for useful biological substances, or reprogramming the human body and mind with genetic or neurobiological engineering. Who can sustain an objection if these practices will help us live longer and with less overt suffering?

It turns out that even the more modest biogenetic engineers, whether they know it or not, are in the immortality business, proceeding on the basis of a quasi-religious faith that all innovation is by definition progress, no matter what is sacrificed to attain it.

Leon Kass, *Commentary*, Spring 1999.

Charles Krauthammer recently wrote about experiments at the University of Texas in which headless mice were created, and raised the specter of headless humans used as organ factories: "there is no grosser corruption of biotechnology than creating a human mutant and disemboweling it for spare parts." Actually, there is perhaps one grosser corruption, for the "headless human" scenario is still a science fiction nightmare: it is much easier to delete mouse genes (preventing the head from growing) than human genes. In the meantime, cloned organs would probably have to develop within human fetuses, which would be aborted when the organs were ready.

This is called "organ farming": growing human life as material. Advocates of cloning like to sidestep the idea of organ farming with visions of growing organs, not a fetus. Such techniques, while theoretically possible, are entirely speculative. There is no reason to believe they will ever be perfected. And, in any case, work with higher-order animals (not banned in any of the bills) would allow such research to continue.

An Affront to the Dignity of Human Reproduction

The infertility applications of cloning have nightmares of their own. Consider: a woman wants "biological" children, but her ovaries do not work because of age or other reasons. She clones herself. The fetus will be female, and have inside her ovaries a lifetime supply of eggs, exactly identical to the woman's own eggs. The fetus is then aborted and the eggs harvested for implantation in the woman. This is an option actually entertained by some fertility doctors, who say they already see a market for it; cloning defenders like Professor Silver celebrate this as a marvelous extension of a woman's reproductive capabilities.

The fact that people are already inventing—and endorsing—such scenarios demonstrates the corrosive magic this technology works on the notion of human dignity. Indeed, it is not just the horrific applications but cloning itself that are abominations. For human beings are unavoidably defined by our biological, embodied natures. How we come into being is not trivial: it is central to who we are. This is one of the reasons why incest, even consensual incest—which like cloning, has no "victims"—offends us to our core. It blurs the lines of kinship: the begotten couples with her begetter.

And if incest crosses the boundaries defined by the human

way of coming into being, cloning twists and breaks them. Parents and children would be replaced with "donors" and "clones." The relationship between the parties to asexual reproduction would be inherently ambiguous (the species which currently practice it, amoebas and the like, show zero interest in their relatives). But that relationship surely would be affected by the fact that cloning constitutes the manufacture of humans as made-to-order goods. The danger is that if people are made and not begotten, they become like everything else which is but a tool: a means, not an end.

Some writers, like Harvard biology professor Richard Lewontin, say all the furor is over nothing. Clones are no different from twins, they say, so what's the big deal? Well, what was the last pair of twins heard of born fifty years apart to two different women? What woman who gives birth to a handsome child can go to a doctor and request another genetically identical one, or maybe a dozen? The real moral issue is not the genetic makeup of clones, but the method of their manufacture. It is asexual reproduction that robs a cloned child of parents, not the fact that someone else shares his genotype.

A Harmful Technology

Some people, of course, have no patience for arguments about morality and justice, and care only about ruddy, healthy human beings. But even they should reject cloning. In individual cases, cloning may benefit some, but it will be a very selfish advance because in the long run it undermines the advancement of the human species. There is good reason that all higher life forms are reproduced through random combinations of two mates' DNA. The constant changes in genotype create the variety necessary for the species to respond to environmental changes. Since the environment is constantly changing, failure to vary the genotype creates genetic stagnation that can be catastrophic.

We've become accustomed to revolutionary technologies emerging daily, from microchips to surgical lasers. But even the most advanced technologies merely facilitate or improve upon normal human functions. While cloning may look just like a particularly impressive piece of laboratory wizardry, actually it redefines the parameters of human life. Such break-throughs do not happen every day.

However, one thing we can say about cloning is that it is an entirely new transgression. Unfortunately, since Eve was beguiled by the serpent, mankind has never been good at understanding sin without experiencing it.

Periodical Bibliography

The following articles have been selected to supplement the diverse views presented in this chapter. Addresses are provided for periodicals not indexed in the *Readers' Guide to Periodical Literature*, the *Alternative Press Index*, the *Social Sciences Index*, or the *Index to Legal Periodicals and Books*.

W. French Anderson	"A Cure That May Cost Us Ourselves," *Newsweek*, January 1, 2000.
Kathryn Sergeant Brown	"Mending Broken Genes," *Popular Science*, October 1999.
Miriam Karmel Feldman	"Is DNA Destiny?: The Ethics of Genetic Screening," *Utne Reader*, March/April 1998.
Nancy Gibbs	"If We Have It, Do We Use It?" *Time*, September 13, 1999.
Issues and Controversies On File	"Cloning," April 18, 1997.
Leon R. Kass	"The Moral Meaning of Genetic Technology," *Commentary*, Spring 1999.
Ellen Licking	"Gene Therapy: One Family's Story," *Business Week*, July 12, 1999.
Robert G. Mckinnell and Marie A. Di Berardino	"The Biology of Cloning: History and Rationale," *BioScience*, November 1999.
Alanna Mitchell	"Now, Genetic Screening for Embryos," *World Press Review*, December 1997.
Stephen G. Post	"The Judeo-Christian Case Against Human Cloning," *America*, June 21, 1997.
Matthew A. Rarey	"Sliding into Eugenics?" *Insight on the News*, November 22, 1999.
Gurney Williams III	"Altered States," *American Legion Magazine*, October 1997.
Ian Wilmut	"Cloning for Medicine," *Scientific American*, December 1998.

How Does Genetic Engineering Affect Food and Agriculture?

Chapter Preface

According to a July 1999 *U.S. News & World Report*, "It is now virtually impossible for Americans to avoid eating genetically modified organisms, or GMOs, as they're often called. Bioengineered corn and soybeans in particular are used as ingredients in a wide range of processed food, from soft drinks and beer to breakfast cereal. They are also fed to farm animals. Even products found in health-food stores, such as tofu and canola oil, often contain genetically modified ingredients."

In Europe, genetically modified foods have been a controversial topic for years. The European Union (EU) has blocked the importation of some genetically altered crops, and since 1997 has required that such foods be specially labeled. In 1999 French protestors brought more attention to the issue when they piled manure in front of several McDonald's restaurants to protest U.S. acceptance of genetically modified foods.

Various theories have been proposed to explain why Americans have accepted genetic engineering in agriculture while Europeans have not. One explanation is that, because Europe has fewer wilderness areas, Europeans are more resistant to technologies that may harm the environment. Another interpretation is that the outcry against genetically engineered food is just part of a trade war between the United States and the EU, with European farmers not wanting to compete with their U.S. counterparts. Still another possibility is that Americans have simply been unaware of the degree to which biotechnology and agriculture have become intertwined in recent years; the protests in France and the trade disagreements with the EU may change that.

The authors in the following chapter examine the two principal, conflicting claims about genetically modified foods: that they are a threat to human health and the environment or that they are the world's greatest hope for dramatically increasing the global food supply.

| "Genetic engineering of food and fiber
| products is inherently unpredictable
| and dangerous."

Genetically Engineered Food Is Dangerous

Ronnie Cummins

Ronnie Cummins is national director of the BioDemocracy Campaign (formerly the Campaign for Food Safety), a grass-roots organization that promotes organic food and opposes genetic engineering in agriculture. In the following viewpoint, Cummins argues that genetic engineering of crops can result in foods that are toxic, carcinogenic, and allergenic. She warns that widespread planting of genetically engineered crops could cause unexpected harm to the environment; as crops are engineered to be resistant to weeds, insects, and viruses, evolution will drive these pests to become stronger and more dangerous. She concludes by calling for a world-wide moratorium on genetic engineering in agriculture.

As you read, consider the following questions:
1. According to the author, how did genetic engineering result in the deaths of thirty-seven Americans in 1989?
2. What percentage of crops planted in 1998 does the author say were genetically engineered to be herbicide resistant?
3. What did Cornell University researchers discover about corn that was genetically engineered to produce the pesticide Bt, according to Cummins?

Reprinted from Ronnie Cummins, "Hazards of Genetically Engineered Food and Crops: Why We Need a Global Moratorium," from the BioDemocracy website. Reprinted with permission from Organic Consumers Association and BioDemocracy Campaign.

The technology of genetic engineering (GE), wielded by transnational "life science" corporations such as Monsanto and Novartis, is the practice of altering or disrupting the genetic blueprints of living organisms—plants, animals, humans, microorganisms—patenting them, and then selling the resulting gene-foods, seeds, or other products for profit. Life science corporations proclaim, with great fanfare, that their new products will make agriculture sustainable, eliminate world hunger, cure disease, and vastly improve public health. In reality, through their business practices and political lobbying, the gene engineers have made it clear that they intend to use GE to dominate and monopolize the global market for seeds, foods, fiber, and medical products.

The Need for a Global Moratorium on Genetic Engineering in Agriculture

GE is a revolutionary new technology still in its early experimental stages of development. This technology has the power to break down fundamental genetic barriers—not only between species—but between humans, animals, and plants. By randomly inserting together the genes of non-related species—utilizing viruses, antibiotic-resistant genes, and bacteria as vectors, markers, and promoters—and permanently altering their genetic codes, gene-altered organisms are created that pass these genetic changes onto their offspring through heredity. Gene engineers all over the world are now snipping, inserting, recombining, rearranging, editing, and programming genetic material. Animal genes and even human genes are randomly inserted into the chromosomes of plants, fish, and animals, creating heretofore unimaginable transgenic life forms. For the first time in history, transnational biotechnology corporations are becoming the architects and "owners" of life.

With little or no regulatory restraints, labeling requirements, or scientific protocol, bio-engineers have begun creating hundreds of new GE "Frankenfoods" and crops, oblivious to human and environmental hazards, or negative socioeconomic impacts on the world's several billion farmers and rural villagers. Despite an increasing number of scientists warning that current gene-splicing techniques are crude, inexact,

110

and unpredictable—and therefore inherently dangerous—pro-biotech governments and regulatory agencies, led by the US, maintain that GE foods and crops are "substantially equivalent" to conventional foods, and therefore require neither mandatory labeling nor pre-market safety-testing. This Brave New World of Frankenfoods is frightening. There are currently more than four dozen genetically engineered foods and crops being grown or sold in the US.

These foods and crops are widely dispersed into the food chain and the environment. Over 60 million acres of GE crops are presently under cultivation in the US, while up to 500,000 dairy cows are being injected regularly with Monsanto's recombinant Bovine Growth Hormone (rBGH). Most supermarket processed food items now "test positive" for the presence of GE ingredients. In addition several dozen more GE crops are in the final stages of development and will soon be released into the environment and sold in the marketplace. According to the biotechnology industry almost 100% of US food and fiber will be genetically engineered within 5–10 years. The "hidden menu" of these unlabeled genetically engineered foods and food ingredients in the US now includes soybeans, soy oil, corn, potatoes, squash, canola oil, cotton seed oil, papaya, tomatoes, and dairy products.

Genetic engineering of food and fiber products is inherently unpredictable and dangerous—for humans, for animals, the environment, and for the future of sustainable and organic agriculture. As Dr. Michael Antoniou, a British molecular scientist points out, gene-splicing has already resulted in the "unexpected production of toxic substances . . . in genetically engineered bacteria, yeast, plants, and animals with the problem remaining undetected until a major health hazard has arisen." The hazards of GE foods and crops fall basically into three categories: human health hazards, environmental hazards, and socioeconomic hazards. A brief look at the already-proven and likely hazards of GE products provides a convincing argument for why we need a global moratorium on all GE foods and crops.

Toxins and Poisons. Genetically engineered products clearly have the potential to be toxic and a threat to human health.

In 1989 a genetically engineered brand of L-tryptophan, a common dietary supplement, killed 37 Americans and permanently disabled or afflicted more than 5,000 others with a potentially fatal and painful blood disorder, eosinophilia myalgia syndrome (EMS), before it was recalled by the Food and Drug Administration. The manufacturer, Showa Denko, Japan's third largest chemical company, had for the first time in 1988–89 used GE bacteria to produce the over-the-counter supplement. It is believed that the bacteria somehow became contaminated during the recombinant DNA process. Showa Denko has already paid out over $2 billion in damages to EMS victims.

Tom Toles ©1999 The Buffalo News. Reprinted with permission of Universal Press Syndicate. All rights reserved.

In 1999, front-page headline stories in the British press revealed Rowett Institute scientist Dr. Arpad Pusztai's explosive research findings that GE potatoes, spliced with DNA from the snowdrop plant and a commonly used viral promoter, the Cauliflower Mosaic Virus (CaMv), are poisonous to mammals. GE-snowdrop potatoes, found to be significantly different in chemical composition from regular potatoes, damaged the vital organs and immune systems of lab rats fed the GE potatoes. Most alarming of all, damage to the rats' stomach linings—apparently a severe viral infection—most likely was caused by the CaMv viral promoter, a promoter spliced into nearly all GE foods and crops.

Dr. Pusztai's pathbreaking research work unfortunately remains incomplete (government funding was cut off and he was fired after he spoke to the media). But more and more scientists around the world are warning that genetic manipulation can increase the levels of natural plant toxins or allergens in foods (or create entirely new toxins) in unexpected ways by switching on genes that produce poisons. And since regulatory agencies do not currently require the kind of thorough chemical and feeding tests that Dr. Pusztai was conducting, consumers have now become involuntary guinea pigs in a vast genetic experiment. As Dr. Pusztai warns, "Think of William Tell shooting an arrow at a target. Now put a blindfold on the man doing the shooting and that's the reality of the genetic engineer doing a gene insertion."

Increased Cancer Risks. In 1994, the FDA approved the sale of Monsanto's controversial GE recombinant Bovine Growth Hormone (rBGH)—injected into dairy cows to force them to produce more milk—even though scientists warned that significantly higher levels (400–500% or more) of a potent chemical hormone, Insulin-Like Growth Factor (IGF-1), in the milk and dairy products of injected cows, could pose serious hazards for human breast, prostate, and colon cancer. A number of studies have shown that humans with elevated levels of IGF-1 in their bodies are much more likely to get cancer. In addition the US Congressional watchdog agency, the GAO, told the FDA not to approve rBGH, arguing that increased antibiotic residues in the milk of rBGH-injected cows (resulting from higher rates of udder infections requiring antibiotic treatment) posed an unacceptable risk for public health. In 1998, heretofore undisclosed Monsanto/FDA documents were released by government scientists in Canada, showing damage to laboratory rats fed dosages of rBGH. Significant infiltration of rBGH into the prostate of the rats as well as thyroid cysts indicated potential cancer hazards from the drug. Subsequently the government of Canada banned rBGH in early 1999. The European Union has had a ban in place since 1994. Although rBGH continues to be injected into 4–5% of all US dairy cows, no other industrialized country has legalized its use. Even the GATT Codex Alimentarius, a United Nations food standards body, has refused to certify that rBGH is safe.

Food Allergies. In 1996 a major GE food disaster was narrowly averted when Nebraska researchers learned that a Brazil nut gene spliced into soybeans could induce potentially fatal allergies in people sensitive to Brazil nuts. Animal tests of these Brazil nut–spliced soybeans had turned up negative. People with food allergies (which currently afflicts 8% of all American children), whose symptoms can range from mild unpleasantness to sudden death, may likely be harmed by exposure to foreign proteins spliced into common food products. Since humans have never before eaten most of the foreign proteins now being gene-spliced into foods, stringent pre-market safety-testing (including long-term animal feeding and volunteer human feeding studies) is necessary in order to prevent a future public health disaster. Mandatory labeling is also necessary so that those suffering from food allergies can avoid hazardous GE foods and so that public health officials can trace allergens back to their source when GE-induced food allergies break out.

Damage to Food Quality and Nutrition. A 1999 study by Dr. Marc Lappe published in the *Journal of Medicinal Food* found that concentrations of beneficial phytoestrogen compounds thought to protect against heart disease and cancer were lower in genetically modified soybeans than in traditional strains. These and other studies, including Dr. Pusztai's, indicate that genetically engineering food will likely result in foods lower in quality and nutrition. For example the milk from cows injected with rBGH contains higher levels of pus, bacteria, and fat.

Antibiotic Resistance. When gene engineers splice a foreign gene into a plant or microbe, they often link it to another gene, called an antibiotic resistance marker gene (ARM), that helps determine if the first gene was successfully spliced into the host organism. Some researchers warn that these ARM genes might unexpectedly recombine with disease-causing bacteria or microbes in the environment or in the guts of animals or people who eat GE food, contributing to the growing public health danger of antibiotic resistance—of infections that cannot be cured with traditional antibiotics, for example new strains of salmonella, e-coli, campylobacter, and enterococci. EU authorities are currently considering a ban on all GE foods containing antibiotic-resistant marker genes.

Dangers to the Environment

Increased Pesticide Residues. Contrary to biotech industry propaganda, recent studies have found that US farmers growing GE crops are using just as many toxic pesticides and herbicides as conventional farmers, and in some cases are using more. Crops genetically engineered to be herbicide-resistant account for 70% of all GE crops planted in 1998. The so-called "benefits" of these herbicide-resistant crops are that farmers can spray as much of a particular herbicide on their crops as they want—killing the weeds without damaging their crop. Scientists estimate that herbicide-resistant crops planted around the globe will triple the amount of toxic broad-spectrum herbicides used in agriculture. These broad-spectrum herbicides are designed to literally kill everything green. The leaders in biotechnology are the same giant chemical companies—Monsanto, DuPont, AgrEvo, Novartis, and Rhone-Poulenc—that sell toxic pesticides. These companies are genetically engineering plants to be resistant to herbicides that they manufacture so they can sell more herbicides to farmers who, in turn, can apply more poisonous herbicides to crops to kill weeds.

Genetic Pollution. "Genetic pollution" and collateral damage from GE field crops already have begun to wreak environmental havoc. Wind, rain, birds, bees, and insect pollinators have begun carrying genetically-altered pollen into adjoining fields, polluting the DNA of crops of organic and non-GE farmers. An organic farm in Texas has been contaminated with genetic drift from GE crops on a nearby farm and EU regulators are considering setting an "allowable limit" for genetic contamination of non-GE foods, because they don't believe genetic pollution can be controlled. Because they are alive, gene-altered crops are inherently more unpredictable than chemical pollutants—they can reproduce, migrate, and mutate. Once released, it is virtually impossible to recall genetically engineered organisms back to the laboratory or the field.

Damage to Beneficial Insects and Soil Fertility. In 1999, Cornell University researchers made a startling discovery. They found that pollen from genetically engineered Bt corn was poisonous to Monarch butterflies. The study adds to a growing body of evidence that GE crops are adversely affecting a number of beneficial insects, including ladybugs and lacewings, as well as beneficial soil microorganisms, bees, and possibly birds.

Dangerous Surprises

Creation of GE "Superweeds" and "Superpests." Genetically engineering crops to be herbicide-resistant or to produce their own pesticide presents dangerous problems. Pests and weeds will inevitably emerge that are pesticide- or herbicide-resistant, which means that stronger, more toxic chemicals will be needed to get rid of the pests. We are already seeing the emergence of the first "superweeds" as GE herbicide-resistant crops such as rapeseed (canola) spread their herbicide-resistance traits to related weeds such as wild mustard plants. Lab and field tests also indicate that common plant pests such as cotton boll worms, living under constant pressure from GE crops, will soon evolve into "superpests" completely immune to Bt sprays and other environmentally sustainable biopesticides. This will present a serious danger for organic and sustainable farmers whose biological pest management practices will be unable to cope with increasing numbers of superpests and superweeds.

Creation of New Viruses and Pathogens. Gene-splicing will inevitably result in unanticipated outcomes and dangerous surprises that damage plants and the environment. Researchers conducting experiments at Michigan State University several years ago found that genetically altering plants to resist viruses can cause the viruses to mutate into new, more virulent forms. Scientists in Oregon found that a genetically engineered soil microorganism, Klebsiella planticola, completely killed essential soil nutrients. Environmental Protection Agency whistle blowers issued similar warnings in 1997 protesting government approval of a GE soil bacteria called Rhizobium melitoli.

Genetic "Bio-Invasion." By virtue of their "superior" genes, some genetically engineered plants and animals will inevitably run amok, overpowering wild species in the same way that introduced exotic species, such as kudzu vine and Dutch elm disease, which have created problems in North America. What will happen to wild fish and marine species, for example, when scientists release into the environment carp, salmon, and trout that are twice as large, and eat twice as much food, as their wild counterparts?

Unethical Technologies

Socioeconomic Hazards. The patenting of genetically engineered foods and widespread biotech food production threatens to eliminate farming as it has been practiced for 12,000 years. GE patents such as the Terminator Technology will render seeds infertile and force hundreds of millions of farmers who now save and share their seeds to purchase evermore expensive GE seeds and chemical inputs from a handful of global biotech/seed monopolies. If the trend is not stopped, the patenting of transgenic plants and food-producing animals will soon lead to universal "bioserfdom" in which farmers will lease their plants and animals from biotech conglomerates such as Monsanto and pay royalties on seeds and offspring. Family and indigenous farmers will be driven off the land and consumers' food choices will be dictated by a cartel of transnational corporations. Rural communities will be devastated. Hundreds of millions of farmers and agricultural workers worldwide will lose their livelihoods.

Ethical Hazards. The genetic engineering and patenting of animals reduces living beings to the status of manufactured products. A purely reductionist science, biotechnology reduces all life to bits of information (genetic code) that can be arranged and rearranged at whim. Stripped of their integrity and sacred qualities, animals who are merely objects to their "inventors" will be treated as such. Currently, hundreds of genetically engineered "freak" animals are awaiting patent approval from the federal government. One can only wonder, after the wholesale gene-altering and patenting of animals, will GE "designer babies" be next?

The Anti–Genetic Engineering Campaign

As the anti–genetic engineering campaign in Europe has shown, mass grassroots action is the key to stopping this technology and moving agriculture in an organic and sustainable direction. The Campaign for Food Safety and the Organic Consumers Association—along with allied organizations and networks worldwide—endorse the following Food Agenda 2000 as the foundation for our local-to-global campaign work:

(1) A Global Moratorium on all Genetically Engineered Foods and Crops;

(2) Stop Factory Farming. Begin the phase-out of industrial agriculture and factory farming—with a goal of significantly reducing the use of toxic chemicals and animal drugs on conventional farms by the year 2010. This phase-out will include a ban on the most dangerous farm chemicals and animal feed additives (antibiotics, hormones, and rendered animal protein) as well as the implementation of intensive Integrated Pest Management Practices (reduce use of toxic pesticides and chemical fertilizers through natural composting, crop rotation, cover crops, use of beneficial insects, etc.).

(3) 30% Organic by the Year 2010. We demand government funding and implementation of transition to organic programs so that at least 30% of US (and global) agriculture is organic by the Year 2010—with a strong emphasis on production for local and regional markets by small and medium-sized organic farmers.

"There is no scientific difference between plants transformed by traditional methods and those transformed by transgene engineering."

Genetically Engineered Food Is Not Dangerous

Thomas R. DeGregori

Thomas R. DeGregori is a professor of economics at the University of Houston. In the following viewpoint, he maintains that the use of genetic engineering and other biotechnologies in agriculture promises to dramatically increase food production. The author believes that movements to ban or put special labels on genetically modified (GM) food are "pandering to hysteria." There is no scientific basis for claims that such foods are harmful to human health or the environment, he writes. In DeGregori's view, the opposition to genetic engineering in agriculture is part of a larger effort among environmentalists to attack technological progress in general.

As you read, consider the following questions:

1. According to the author, what socioeconomic groups benefit most from the use of biotechnology in medicine, and what groups are most in need of genetically modified foods?
2. What evidence does the author cite to rebuke the claim that corn engineered to produce Bt toxin harms Monarch butterflies?
3. In DeGregori's opinion, what would the labeling of genetically modified foods imply to consumers?

Excerpted from Thomas R. DeGregori, *Modern Agriculture and Technology: A Defense* (Ames: Iowa State University Press, 2000). Reprinted by permission of the author.

For over two decades, biotechnology has been an effective means of creating new pharmaceuticals or mass producing known drugs that were previously difficult and expensive to produce and limited in availability. As such, it was a proven method for bettering the human condition. . . .

By the 1990s, the biotechnology for inserting a gene for a specific trait was increasingly being used in agricultural research for crops like cotton, maize and soybeans. Even though testing for safety and prior approval were not required for crops from traditional plant breeding, a testing and approval process was worked out through co-operation between the private and public sectors. The new seeds were marketed to farmers and their crops entered the marketplace virtually unnoticed by the public. . . . As the number of people using or consuming these products mounted into the hundreds of millions, there were not and subsequently have not been any adverse human health outcomes, verifiable or otherwise, in their production, processing, use or consumption.

By the mid-1990s, bioengineered crops were being grown in such diverse places as Argentina, France, China and India as well as the United States and Canada. Large acreage for many other experimental bioengineered crops could be found in these and other countries. Experimentation and testing for safety was not only taking place in the field but others in the private, public and non-governmental and professional sectors were studying and examining the issues involved in bioengineering from every conceivable perspective including ethics and religion with bioengineering passing all with flying colors. . . .

The War over Bioengineered Foods

The very vastness of the knowledge involved in modern science and technology makes it impossible for all of us to know everything or even everything that we "need" to know. So it is not condescending to say that the public was largely uniformed about biotechnology in spite of occasional favorable popular articles over the previous two decades. This allowed with the most profound ignorance such as Jeremy Rifkin, Greenpeace or Friends of the Earth to dominate the inevitable and necessary public discourse. They scored early with their misinformation by defining the terms of discussion with such names as frankenfoods and terminator genes. They played both sides of the "science" game. When a study in the UK that was not peer reviewed was released in a press conference and on television purported to show the dangers of bioengineered crops, they claimed that science was on their side. When the leading scientists countered that these conclusions were unwarranted and that bioengineered foodstuffs were safe, then we were told that scientists were not to be trusted; after all, look at the mad cow scare in the UK and the way that the scientists allegedly misled the public. All of which is to say that science is "good" when it confirms Luddite fears and "bad" when it denies them. In the public arena, ideologues can pronounce on issues with a confident air of certainty while scientific inquiry is by its very nature dealing with subtle detail and operates in terms of probabilities and not certainties. . . .

The war over bioengineered foods is well under way. In the United Kingdom, continental Europe and in other parts of the world, much of the public, if not a majority, have been thoroughly brainwashed on this issue and frightened to the point of opposition to all uses of bioengineering in agriculture. Many political leaders in Europe who should know better are pandering to the hysteria rather than trying to educate and provide enlightened, intelligent leadership for their citizens. Though the public in the United States has not yet been aroused on the issue, the vandals are in the fields tearing up the crops and the organized opposition is growing as the United States has to deal with those who are trying to use issues of bioengineered foods as a way of restraining trade. The effort of many pharmaceutical companies to rid themselves of their agricultural divisions and the response of investors to biotechnology firms—pharmaceuticals without agriculture going up—sends a danger signal that we can not ignore.

In many ways, the first battle of this war has gone to those who oppose modern science and technology. The following viewpoint dwells on the specifics of the biotechnology issue but this issue is part of the ongoing conflict between unreason and reason, between those who seek progress for all and those who operate in a make-believe new age world. . . .

Many botanists find the opposition to genetically modified plants to be irrational. Plant scientists cite statements by the National Academy of Sciences and by 11 scientific societies that insist that there is no scientific difference between plants transformed by traditional methods and those transformed by transgene engineering.

These scientists make the intelligent, pragmatic argument that "safety and acceptability should be decided on a plant by plant basis, not by the method that produced the plant.". . .

Genetic Engineering in Medicine Is Widely Accepted

The row over genetically modified foods also contrasts oddly with the widespread acceptance and use of many recombinant products in health care. These include human insulin and growth hormone, erythropoietin, hepatitis B vaccine, tissue plasminogen activator, several interferons, factor VIII, and antihemophilic factor.

[Bernard Dixon writes,] "In the United Kingdom, many people welcome medical applications of gene technology as 'good genetics' but see genetically modified foods as 'bad genetics.'" Over "25% of the top 20 drugs, for example insulin, growth hormone, several hepatitis B vaccines, and monoclonal antibodies to treat cancer" are produced using genetically modified organisms. Florence Wambugu asks "why there should be different standards for crops and pharmaceuticals, particularly in Africa where the need for food is crucial for survival?". . .

What is also being ignored is the fact the many trade regulations now in place in developed countries because of pressure from environmental groups and NGOs [nongovernmental organizations], end up restricting the export of products (such as a new vaccine) that are *wanted* by developing and other recipient countries.

Concomitant with the debate over genetically modified foods, articles are being posted on the same websites (BBC for example) on genetic modifications to produce a vaccine for the plague and another to introduce a human gene into cows so that they produce a protein which could be useful for treating multiple sclerosis. Neither these or other use of the genetic modification technology seem to cause the controversy that genetic modification of foods does. The main beneficiaries of recombinant products in health care are the middle and upper income groups in developed countries from whose ranks come most of the protestors against genetically modified foods. Excluded from the debate on genetically modified foods are those most in need of increased food production, the poor in developing countries and the "largely marginalized" hungry in developed countries. . . .

Frankenfoods or Frankenfears?
The Butterfly Scare

Critics use the term, "Frankenstein foods" or "Frankenfoods" and "mutant grub" to describe the food products of genetic engineering. The *New Scientist* calls this terminology, "Frankenfears." In the United States, "65 plaintiffs including Greenpeace, the Sierra Club and the International Federation of Organic Agriculture Movements" are suing the Environmental Protection Agency (EPA) arguing that it was unlawful for the EPA to approve genetically modified crops that produce Bt toxin, a toxin that is "naturally" produced by the bacterium, Bacillus thuringiensis.

Widely circulated in the media have been reports that the Bt-modified plants threatened the continued existence of Monarch butterflies but the solid, scientific criticism of that thesis was largely ignored by the media. Two researchers found it "surprising . . . that a previous and more relevant and realistic field study" was "largely overlooked by the media." Also not widely publicized by the media was the fact the study was admittedly "preliminary rather than definite" as noted by other scientists who otherwise praised the study. Being that the study was preliminary, critics found numerous problems with it without otherwise faulting its merits.

The results were based on the laboratory feeding of Monarch butterfly larvae with leaves from milkweed plants (the larvae's food of choice) that had been dusted with the pollen from a Bt hybrid maize (corn) without their being a field study. The actual field studies—"ongoing monitoring"—of Bt crops found that the pollen diminished rapidly "only 3 meters from the corn field's edge." John Losey, the lead author of the report in *Nature*, found in field studies that the Monarch butterflies avoided "laying eggs on milkweed planted near corn fields." It was also found that corn pollination was "95 percent complete by the time the first monarch eggs began hatching" and that "90 percent of the Bt corn pollen lands within 15 feet of the edge of the corn field." In any case, the 1999 Bt corn crop, about 30% of all U.S. corn acreage, seems not to have harmed the Monarch butterfly as it seems to be a good year for them as measured by the numbers arriving in Mexican sanctuaries. . . .

Genetically Engineered Crops Are More Resistant to Disease

To its credit, the British Broadcasting Corporation (BBC) did post a story on its web page noting a study that showed that "health risks" were "reduced by GM corn" but unfortunately if any other major media picked up the story, it was not sufficiently prominent to be found by a search of their web posting. The GM corn "has a distinct health benefit of discouraging the buildup of mycotoxins in corn, potentially dangerous human and animal toxins produced by fungi that cause plant disease."

Insects that damage plants also both make them more receptive to disease invasion and serve as carriers for these disease pathogens. [The American Phytopathological Society explains] "Insect larvae chew on stalks and kernels, creating wounds where fungal spores can enter the plant. Once established, these fungi often produce mycotoxins." Some mycotoxins such as the fumonisins "can be fatal to horses and pigs, and are probable human carcinogens." The fumonisins are associated with Fusarium ear rot which is the most common ear rot disease in the Corn Belt; it can be found in nearly every cornfield at harvest. The Bt-modified maize (corn) in resisting insect damage from corn borers also helps to protect against disease invasion as well. . . .

The Folly of Calls to Ban, Label, or Place Restrictions on Genetically Modified Food

Many of those in Britain such as Friends of the Earth who are calling for a "moratorium" on the production and use of

genetically modified foods, or Greenpeace who are demanding a prior agreement between countries in order for there to be international trade in genetically modified foods, are being less than fully candid. If these organizations can not get the genetically modified foods banned, then they demand that they be so labeled. In principle, few could object to some form of labeling or a "prior informed consent" type of arrangement (with the emphasis on "informed," not merely sharing phobias), provided it is not simply a ploy to mire the process in bureaucracy and significantly raise the cost of the food. After all, one of the many purposes of genetic modification of food crops is to increase production and lower the cost, making food more available to the needy. Certainly, there would be no objection if private groups wish to ban together to establish standards and organize their own labeling. This is done all the time by religious groups who set standards and arrange for labeling as Kosher or non-Kosher or Halal or non-Halal. Government is and should not be involved in the process except in case of fraudulent labeling. The religious groups neither seek nor would they welcome government involvement in a process that has little if any meaning to the rest of the community. We may have the very highest respect for other people's religious beliefs and the dietary practices that follow from them but we share with the believers that this is a private matter as it should also be for the anti-technology true believers and their desire for labeling.

The consensus is and has been that labeling is for objective, scientific information that is of use to all consumers. In the context of the current debate over genetically modified foodstuffs, labeling would imply that there is a scientifically verifiable difference in terms of health and nutrition when there is not. It would serve to validate the arguments of the opponents of genetic modification in the minds of the public even though the opponents have failed to do so in the scientific journals. As a practical matter, it is simply impossible to accommodate on food labels the personal preferences of every religious, ethnic or other groups that have dietary prohibitions. Basic information is provided to everyone and the rest is up to each group. To require labels to state "GM" or "GM free" makes no more sense than to require all labels to state that they are kosher or non-kosher. . . .

Both a moratorium and restrictions on trade would simply provide greater opportunity for those opposed to genetically modified foods to whip up more hysteria in an effort to have them banned completely. These same groups argue, on the international trade debate for full disclosure and prior approval on genetically modified foods, that it is also an issue of consumer choice. It is an ironic, if not hypocritical use of language that banning a product that others of us wish to consume and for which there is no *verifiable scientific evidence of harm to humans* is not a restriction of choice, but highly bureaucratic procedures for international trade in food, which would make it more expensive and therefore less available to those who need it most, somehow enhance free choice.

Safety Testing Is Adequate

There are serious scientific concerns about foodstuffs that have genes that have been inserted from other plants—such as fatal food allergies. Applying the label of "Frankenstein foods" immediately polarizes and trivializes discourse on the issue and makes it difficult, if not impossible, to reach a public understanding and policy formulation that allow us to realize the benefits of the technology and avoid the potentially deleterious outcomes. The regulations in place for genetically modified foods make them one of the most carefully regulated consumer products. Conversely, there is virtually no regulation for crops bred by conventional methods, even though they may pose the same dangers that are alleged for the genetically modified varieties.

In an editorial titled, "Genetically Modified Confusion," the *Washington Post* wisely recognizes that there has to be a "proper balance of safety testing" while also recognizing "a legitimate area for further debate." It adds, however, that "the purpose of such debate should be to improve biotech research and enhance its acceptance, not to stop it in its tracks.". . .

Some GM crops did in fact have the deleterious potential claimed by its opponents. This included crops that had wild progenitors that could have been transformed by the new GM crop and food crops that had the allergenic properties of the transferred gene. But existing procedures identified these difficulties in the testing phase and their development was correctly terminated. The testing procedures worked but they can always be improved but as an outcome of reasoned discourse and not hysteria. Since over 90 percent of food allergies result from "specific proteins in eight foods: peanuts, tree nuts, milk, eggs, soybeans, shell fish, fish and wheat," procedures have been established to require tests for allergenic responses in foodstuffs that have been altered with genes from these sources.

One author argues that rather than being insufficiently tested as the critics claim, genetically modified crops have been subjected to far more testing than would be warranted by any consideration of potential danger. Henry Miller maintains that it was the major developers of GM crops that lobbied in the United States for strict regulation that was costly to the producers as a means of making difficult if not essentially impossible for independent entrepreneurs, small biotech firms and University researchers to compete against them. To Miller, the large firms scored a "Pyrrhic victory" in keeping down competition but thereby "fed the anti-technology mythology that has poisoned views of the consumers." However we may view the "transgressions" of the biotech seed industry, they "pale beside the actions of their ideological opponents." In the process, we are all losers.

Hysteria and Junk Science

The words of Patrick Moore, a green activist and a founder of Greenpeace are instructive. He accuses Greenpeace and other opponents of GM foods of "abandoning science and following agendas that have little to do with saving the earth." Moore cogently argues that:

> I believe we are entering an era now where pagan beliefs and junk science are influencing public policy. GM foods and forestry are both good examples where policy is being influenced by arguments that have no basis in fact or logic.

. . . Clearly, we are at the beginning and not the end of the struggle for GM foods and for the rule of reason and civilized discourse over fear and irrationality. Optimists, like this author, firmly believe that in the long run, the new technology will prevail and humankind will be the better for it but we must use our optimism as a spur to enhanced vigilance and action and not as a basis for complacency. Every delay in the development and dissemination of GM foods will cause more misery and death for those most in need of the benefits of the new technology. We need not adopt the apocalyptic vision of the Luddites to recognize that the stakes in this battle are high and that not only is a pro-GM food outcome essential but that we must move forward as rapidly and judiciously as possible. This is truly a moral crusade and one that we must not lose.

"Genetic modification of crops . . . harnesses the forces of nature to the benefit of feeding the human race."

Genetically Engineered Food Could Help End World Hunger

Norman Borlaug

Norman Borlaug won the Nobel Peace Prize in 1970 for his work in developing high-yield wheat and other grains in India and other Third World nations. His work was a major part of the "Green Revolution" that resulted in dramatically increased worldwide food production in the early 1970s. In the following viewpoint, Borlaug warns that, because of the growing number of people worldwide, new advances in agricultural production are needed to prevent widespread starvation. Borlaug argues that the genetic engineering of crops could be one such breakthrough. He believes that genetically engineering crops is little different from the cross-breeding among plant species that occurs in nature, and he argues that it is irresponsible for affluent environmentalists to prevent these types of foods from reaching developing nations.

As you read, consider the following questions:

1. According to the author, how many tons of food are currently produced per year, and by what year will that number need to nearly double in order to feed the world's population?
2. By what percent might grain yields in North America and Western Europe increase with genetic engineering breakthroughs, according to Borlaug?

Reprinted from Norman Borlaug, "Biotech Can Feed 8 Billion in the Next Century," *New Perspectives Quarterly*, Fall 1999. Reprinted with permission from Blackwell Publishers.

N early 30 years ago, in my acceptance speech for the Nobel Peace Prize, I said that the Green Revolution was a temporary victory in man's war against hunger which, if fully implemented, could provide sufficient food for humankind through the end of the 20th century. But I warned that unless the frightening power of human reproduction was curbed, the success of the Green Revolution would only be ephemeral.

Agricultural science has so far been able to meet food production demands.

But the population monster continues to run amok. During the 1990s alone, world population grew by nearly one billion people and will grow again by another one billion during the first decade of the 21st century. It is projected to reach 8.3 billion by 2025 before stabilizing (hopefully) at about 10 billion toward the end of the next century.

Clearly the most fundamental challenge ahead is to produce and equitably distribute an adequate food supply for this heavily burdened planet.

I believe that we have the agricultural technology—either already available or well-advanced in the research pipeline—to feed those 8.3 billion people anticipated in the next quarter of a century. The more pertinent question today is whether farmers and ranchers will be permitted to use that technology.

Environmental Elitists and the False Promise of Organic Farming

Extremists in the environmental movement from the rich nations seem to be doing everything they can to stop scientific progress in its tracks. Small, but vociferous, highly effective and well-funded Luddites are predicting doom and provoking fear, slowing the application of new technology, whether it be transgenics, biotechnology or more conventional methods of agricultural science. Witness the campaign against genetically modified crops called "Frankenstein food" by activists in Great Britain and elsewhere in Europe.

I am particularly alarmed by those elitists who seek to deny small-scale farmers in the Third World, especially in sub-Saharan Africa, access to conventionally improved seeds, fertilizers and crop-protection chemicals that have allowed the affluent nations the luxury of plentiful and inexpensive foodstuffs which, in turn, has accelerated their economic development.

While the affluent nations can certainly afford to pay more for food produced by so-called "organic" methods, the one billion chronically undernourished people of the low-income, food-deficit nations cannot. (There isn't enough "organic fertilizer" to produce the food for today's population of 6 billion. If we attempted to produce the equivalent of the 80 million tons of nutrient nitrogen from manure needed for such a task, world cattle production would have to increase to 5 or 6 billion head.)

Of course, we must be environmentally responsible. I have always subscribed to what in the old days we used to call "integrated crop management" and is today called "sustainability"—utilizing the land for the greatest good for the greatest number of people over the longest period of time.

But today's extremist thinking is dangerously misguided. Most worrisome, it preys upon a "knowledge gap" about the complexities of biology among the general public in the affluent societies—now thoroughly urban and removed from any relationship to the land—that grows ever greater with the rapid advances in genetics and plant biotechnology.

No doubt one of the other great challenges of the coming century is a renewal and broadening of scientific education—particularly in primary, secondary and early college levels—that keeps pace with the times. Nowhere is it more important for knowledge to confront fear born of ignorance than in this basic activity of mankind—the production of food. The needless confrontation of consumers against the use of transgenic crop technology, now so widespread in Europe and growing in the United States and Asia, could have been avoided with sound education about genetic diversity and variation.

The fact is we cannot turn back the clock on agriculture and only use methods that were developed to feed a much smaller number of people. It took some 10,000 years to expand food production to the current level of about five billion tons per year. By 2025 we will have to nearly double that amount, and that cannot be done unless farmers across the world have access to current high-yield crop-production methods and to continuing biotech breakthroughs.

Nature's Own GM Foods

"Genetically modified organism" (GMO) and "genetically modified food" (GMF) are ambiguous and imprecise terms that have contributed greatly to the fuss over the use of transgenic crops—crops grown from seeds that contain the genes of different species.

But, long before mankind started breeding plants, Mother Nature did. The wheat groups we currently rely on for much of our food supply are the result of natural crosses between different species of grasses.

Today's bread wheat is made up of three different plant genomes, each containing a set of seven chromosomes each. The most primitive wheat types are called "diploids," which still grow wild in their zone of origin in the Near East. Before agriculture was born, diploid wheat crossed with another wild grass and became the first major wheat crop of commerce, which we know as "tetraploids," the durum or pasta wheat. This wheat dates back to the Sumerians from 6,000 B.C. and remained the most important wheat of commerce until well into the Roman period. Then somewhere—no one knows where—the tetraploids crossed with another species of wild grass to produce the bread wheats from which we make leavened bread today.

What probably happened is that a light frost killed the pollen in the male stamen at a temperature just below freezing, but leaving the female receptive. The female stigma exerted itself on the outside of the plant on the feathery end of the stalk, where the pollen from another plant landed. Thus, a new cross species was born. Nature's own "GM food."

Thus, the bread wheat varieties that account for 98 percent of the tonnage of wheat produced today are "transgenic."

Thanks to the development of science in the past couple of centuries, we now have the insights into plant genetics and breeding to do purposefully what Mother Nature herself did in the past by chance or design. Genetic modification of crops is not some kind of witchcraft; like cultivation, it harnesses the forces of nature to the benefit of feeding the human race.

Over the past seven decades, conventional plant breeding has produced vast numbers of improved varieties and hybrids that have contributed immensely to higher grain yield,

Anti-Science Activists Are Irresponsible

Dr. C.S. Prakash, who directs the Center for Plant Biotechnology Research at Tuskegee University in Tuskegee, Alabama, said the following in a column for the *Atlanta Journal-Constitution*:

> Anti-technology activists accuse corporations of "playing God" by genetically improving crops, but it is these so-called environmentalists who are really playing God, not with genes but with the lives of poor and hungry people.

While activist organizations spend hundreds of thousands of dollars to promote fear through anti-science newspaper ads, 1.3 billion people, who live on less than $1 a day, care only about finding their next day's meal. Biotechnology is one of the best hopes for solving their food needs today, when we have 6 billion people, and certainly in the next 30 to 50 years, when there will be 9 billion on the globe.

Those people, who battle weather, pests and plant disease to try to raise enough for their families, can benefit tremendously from biotechnology, and not just from products created by big corporations. Public-sector institutions are conducting work on high-yield rice, virus-resistant sweet potato and more healthful strains for cassava, crops that are staples in developing countries.

The development of local and regional agriculture is the key to addressing both hunger and low income. Genetically improved food is "scale neutral," in that a poor rice farmer with one acre in Bangladesh can benefit as much as a larger farmer in California. And he doesn't have to learn a sophisticated new system; he only has to plant a seed. New rice strains being developed through biotechnology can increase yields by 30 to 40 percent. Another rice strain has the potential to prevent blindness in millions of children whose diets are deficient in Vitamin A.

Edible vaccines, delivered in locally grown crops, could do more to eliminate disease than the Red Cross, missionaries and U.N. task forces combined, at a fraction of the cost. But none of these benefits will be realized if Western-generated fears about biotechnology halt research funding and close borders to exported products.

For the well-fed to spearhead fear-based campaigns and suppress research for ideological and pseudo-science reasons is irresponsible and immoral.

Christopher Bond, *Congressional Record*, January 26, 2000.

stability of harvests and farm income. But there has been no major increase in the maximum genetic yield potential of wheat and rice since the dwarf varieties that gave rise to the Green Revolution of the 1960s and 1970s.

To meet the rapidly growing food needs of the population, we must find new and appropriate technologies to raise cereal crop yields. Recent developments in animal biotechnology have produced Bovine somatatropin (BST), now widely used to increase milk production. Currently, vast commercial areas are planted with transgenic varieties and hybrids of cotton, maize and potatoes that contain genes from *Bacillus thuringiensis*, which effectively control a number of serious insect pests. The use of such varieties will protect crops while greatly reducing the need for insecticide sprays and dusts. Great progress has also been made in development of transgenic plants of cotton, maize, oilseed rape, soybeans, sugarbeet and wheat with tolerance to a number of herbicides. This can lead to a reduction in herbicide use by much more specific dosages and timing of applications.

There are also promising developments of transgenic plants for the control of viral and fungal diseases, especially by employing "virus coat protein" genes in transgenetic varieties of potatoes and rice. Different promising disease-resistant genes are being incorporated into other transgenic crop species. Obviously, the reduction of damage to crops by pestilence and disease increases yield.

Finally, preliminary experiments have shown that inserted genes from some species can help crops withstand drought conditions.

Raising Yield Levels on Existing Lands, New Frontiers

Total global food production now stands at around 5 billion metric tons annually. (Had the world's food supply been distributed evenly in 1994, it would have provided an adequate diet of 2,350 calories per day for a year for 6.4 billion people—about 800 million more than the actual population.)

To meet projected food demands, however, the average yield of all cereals must be increased by 80 percent between now and 2025. Using currently available technologies, yields can still be doubled in much of the Indian sub-Continent, Latin America, the former USSR and Eastern Europe, and by 100–200 percent in sub-Saharan Africa—provided that political stability is maintained, entrepreneurial initiative is let loose and production inputs are made available at the farm level.

Yield gains in industrialized North America and Western Europe will be much harder to achieve since they already have such high levels. Still, with genetic engineering breakthroughs, yields in these areas could increase as much as 20 percent over the next 35 years.

The most frightening prospect of food insecurity is found in sub-Saharan Africa where the number of chronically undernourished people could actually rise to several hundred million people if current trends of declining per capita production are not reversed. Increasing population pressures, extreme poverty, disease and lack of health care, poor education, poor soil, uncertain rainfall, changing ownership patterns for land and cattle and poorly developed infrastructure combine to make agricultural development very difficult.

Despite these challenges, many of the elements that worked in Asia and Latin America during the 1960s and 1970s can also work to bring a Green Revolution to sub-Saharan Africa. An effective system to deliver modern inputs—seeds, fertilizers, crop-protection chemicals—and market output must be established. If this is done, subsistence farmers, who constitute more than 70 percent of the population in most countries there, can have a chance to feed their people.

What about new lands for growing food? The vast acid-soils area found in the Brazilian *cerrado*, or savannah, and *llanos* of Colombia and Venezuela, central and south Africa, and in Indonesia are among the last major land frontiers available for agriculture. As with the Brazilian *cerrado* these lands have historically never been cultivated because their soils were leached of nutrients long before humankind appeared on the planet. These soils are strongly acidic and have toxic levels of soluble aluminum.

Improved crop management systems built in recent years around liming, fertilizing to restore nutrients, crop rotation and minimum tillage have made these lands productive.

Newly developed varieties of aluminum-tolerant soybeans, maize, rice and wheat sorghum are now also being cultivated in these new areas.

By 1990, 20 million tons of rainfed crops were grown on 10 million hectares (out of 100 million potentially arable hectares). By 2010, food production in the *cerrado* is expected to increase to 98 million tons, a fourfold increase over 1990.

Moral Obligation to Warn of Starvation

At the end of the Earth Summit in Rio de Janeiro, over 400 scientists presented an appeal to heads of state and government. That appeal has now been signed by thousands of scientists, including myself. Let me quote the last paragraph:

"The greatest evils which stalk our Earth are ignorance and oppression, and not science, technology and industry, whose instruments, when adequately managed, are indispensable tools of a future shaped by humanity, by itself and for itself, in overcoming major problems like overpopulation, starvation and worldwide diseases."

Agricultural scientists and policy makers have a moral obligation to warn our political, educational and religious leaders about the magnitude and seriousness of the arable land, food and population problems that lie ahead. They must also recognize the indirect effect the huge human population pressures exert on the habitats of many wild species of flora and fauna, pushing them toward extinction.

If we fail to do so in a forthright manner we will be contributing to the pending chaos of incalculable millions of deaths by starvation. The problem will not vanish by itself; to continue to ignore it will make a future solution more difficult to achieve.

| *"The private sector will not develop crops to solve poor people's problems, because there is not enough money in it."*

Genetically Engineered Food Will Not Help End World Hunger

Brian Halweil

Brian Halweil is a staff researcher at the Worldwatch Institute, an organization that works to raise awareness of global environmental issues. In the following viewpoint, Halweil examines the claim that advances in biotechnology will revolutionize agriculture and increase global food production. Halweil argues that engineering crops to be more resistant to pesticides—so that farmers can increase their use of these chemicals—will eventually result in weeds and insects becoming resistant to those chemicals. The author warns that rather than increasing the food supply, bioengineered foods will give biotechnology companies more control over farmers, since these companies will patent and charge higher prices for the new higher-yield crops they develop.

As you read, consider the following questions:

1. According to Halweil, what was the first transgenic crop planted for commercial use?
2. What are the two principal herbicide-resistant crop "technology packages" that are currently sold to farmers, according to the author?
3. In Halweil's opinion, what "biological obstacle" will limit the role biotechnology will play as an "agricultural savior"?

Excerpted from Brian Halweil, "The Emperor's New Crops," *World Watch*, July/August 1999. Reprinted with permission from Worldwatch Institute.

It's June 1998 and Robert Shapiro, CEO of Monsanto Corporation, is delivering a keynote speech at "BIO 98," the annual meeting of the Biotechnology Industry Organization. "Somehow," he says, "we're going to have to figure out how to meet a demand for a doubling of the world's food supply, when it's impossible to conceive of a doubling of the world's acreage under cultivation. And it is impossible, indeed, even to conceive of increases in productivity—using current technologies—that don't produce major issues for the sustainability of agriculture."

Those "major issues" preoccupy a growing number of economists, environmentalists, and other analysts concerned with agriculture. Given the widespread erosion of topsoil, the continued loss of genetic variety in the major crop species, the uncertain effects of long-term agrochemical use, and the chronic hunger that now haunts nearly 1 billion people, it would seem that a major paradigm shift in agriculture is long overdue. Yet Shapiro was anything but gloomy. Noting "the sense of excitement, energy, and confidence" that engulfed the room, he argued that "biotechnology represents a potentially sustainable solution to the issue of feeding people."

To its proponents, biotech is the key to that new agricultural paradigm. They envision crops genetically engineered to tolerate dry, low-nutrient, or salty soils—allowing some of the world's most degraded farmland to flourish once again. Crops that produce their own pesticides would reduce the need for toxic chemicals, and engineering for better nutrition would help the overfed as well as the hungry. In industry gatherings, biotech appears as some rare hybrid between corporate mega-opportunity and international social program.

The roots of this new paradigm were put down nearly 50 years ago, when James Watson and Francis Crick defined the structure of DNA, the giant molecule that makes up a cell's chromosomes. Once the structure of the genetic code was understood, researchers began looking for ways to isolate little snippets of DNA—particular genes—and manipulate them in various ways. In 1973, scientists managed to paste a gene from one microbe into another microbe of a different species; the result was the first artificial transfer of genetic information across the species boundary. In the early 1980s, several research teams—including one at Monsanto, then a multinational pesticide company—succeeded in splicing a bacterium gene into a petunia. The first "transgenic" plant was born.

Such plants represented a quantum leap in crop breeding: the fact that a plant could not interbreed with a bacterium was no longer an obstacle to using the microbe's genes in crop design. Theoretically, at least, the world's entire store of genetic wealth became available to plant breeders, and the biotech labs were quick to test the new possibilities. Among the early creations was a tomato armed with a flounder gene to enhance frost resistance and with a rebuilt tomato gene to retard spoilage. A variety of the oilseed crop known as rape or canola was outfitted with a gene from the California Bay tree to alter the composition of its oil. A potato was endowed with bacterial resistance from a chicken gene.

Transgenic crops are no longer just a laboratory phenomenon. Since 1986, 25,000 transgenic field trials have been conducted worldwide—a full 10,000 of these [since 1997]. More than 60 different crops—ranging from corn to strawberries, from apples to potatoes—have been engineered. From 2 million hectares in 1996, the global area planted in transgenics jumped to 27.8 million hectares in 1998. That's nearly a fifteenfold increase in just two years.

In 1992, China planted out a tobacco variety engineered to resist viruses and became the first nation to grow transgenic crops for commercial use. Farmers in the United States sowed their first commercial crop in 1994; their counterparts in Argentina, Australia, Canada, and Mexico followed suit in 1996. By 1998, nine nations were growing transgenics for market and that number is expected to reach 20 to 25 by 2000.

Ag biotech is now a global phenomenon, but it remains powerfully concentrated in several ways:

In terms of where transgenics are planted. Three-quarters of transgenic cropland is in the United States. More than a third of the U.S. soybean crop last year was transgenic, as was nearly one-quarter of the corn and one-fifth of the cotton. The only other countries with a substantial transgenic harvest are Argentina and Canada: over half of the 1998 Argentine soybean crop was transgenic, as was over half of the Canadian canola crop. These three nations account for 99 percent of global transgenic crop area. (Most countries have been slow to adopt transgenics because of public concern over possible risks to ecological and human health.)

In terms of which crops are in production. While many crops have been engineered, only a very few are cultivated in appreciable quantities. Soybeans account for 52 percent of global transgenic area, corn for another 30 percent. Cotton—almost entirely on U.S. soil—and canola in Canada cover most of the rest.

In terms of which traits are in commercial use. Most of the transgenic harvest has been engineered for "input traits" intended to replace or accommodate the standard chemical "inputs" of large-scale agriculture, especially insecticides and herbicides. Worldwide, nearly 30 percent of transgenic cropland is planted in varieties designed to produce an insect-killing toxin, and almost all of the rest is in crops engineered to resist herbicides. (A crop's inability to tolerate exposure to a particular herbicide will obviously limit the use of that chemical.)

These two types of crops—the insecticidal and the herbicide-resistant varieties—are biotech's first large-scale commercial ventures. They provide the first real opportunity to test the industry's claims to be engineering a new agricultural paradigm.

The Bugs

The only insecticidal transgenics currently in commercial use are "Bt crops." Grown on nearly 8 million hectares worldwide in 1998, these plants have been equipped with a gene from the soil organism *Bacillus thuringiensis* (Bt), which produces a substance that is deadly to certain insects.

The idea behind Bt crops is to free conventional agriculture from the highly toxic synthetic pesticides that have defined pest control since World War II. Shapiro, for instance, speaks of Monsanto's Bt cotton as a way of substituting "information encoded in a gene in a cotton plant for airplanes flying over cotton fields and spraying toxic chemicals on them." (As with other high technologies, the substitution of information for stuff is a fundamental doctrine of biotech.) At least in the short term, Bt varieties have allowed farmers to cut their spraying of insecticide-intensive crops, like cotton and potato. In 1998, for instance, the typical Bt cotton grower in Mississippi sprayed only once for tobacco budworm and cotton bollworm—the insects targeted by Bt— while non-Bt growers averaged five sprayings.

The Wisdom of Traditional Farmers

Throughout history, the greatest agricultural scientist always has been the farmer, whether large or small, whether a technologically advanced producer in Kansas or a family hoeing a few acres in Ethiopia. The farmer is the one with the most at stake, the one who has made farming his way of life and who has learned to work within his environment to the greatest success.

You can't store that information in a gene bank and you can't replicate it in a corporate lab. When you plow under the genetic wealth that is the result of that effort, you replace the time-tested with the brand new. It's exciting, but it's a gamble.

Rather than promoting the spread of American-style mega-farming—however beneficial it has proven—and serving as the de facto marketing arm for U.S. biotechnology, the U.S. Department of Agriculture (USDA) would do better to work more closely with indigenous farmers in developing nations. We would be wise to remember that the local knowledge and lore of indigenous farmers about what seeds grow best where can be as valuable as our high-tech expertise.

Reed Karaim, *Washington Post*, April 11, 1999.

Farmers are buying into this approach in a big way. Bt crops have had some of the highest adoption rates that the seed industry has ever seen for new varieties. In the United States, just a few years after commercialization, nearly 25 percent of the corn crop and 20 percent of the cotton crop is Bt. In some counties in the southeastern states, the adoption rate of Bt cotton has reached 70 percent. The big draw for farmers is a lowering of production costs from reduced insecticide spraying, although the savings is partly offset by the more expensive seed. . . .

Unfortunately, there is a systemic problem in the background that will almost certainly erode these gains: pesticide resistance. Modern pest management tends to be very narrowly focused; the idea, essentially, is that when faced with a problematic pest, you should look for a chemical to kill it. The result has been a continual toughening of the pests, which has rendered successive generations of chemicals useless. After more than 50 years of this evolutionary rivalry, there is abundant evidence that pests of all sorts—insects, weeds, or pathogens—will develop resistance to just about any chemical that humans throw at them.

The Bt transgenics basically just replace an insecticide that is sprayed on the crop with one that is packaged inside it. The technique may be more sophisticated but the strategy remains the same: aim the chemical at the pest. Some entomologists are predicting that, without comprehensive strategies to prevent it, pest resistance to Bt could appear in the field within three to five years of widespread use, rendering the crops ineffective. Widespread resistance to Bt would affect more than the transgenic crops, since Bt is also commonly used in conventional spraying. Farmers could find one of their most environmentally benign pesticides beginning to slip away.

In one respect, Bt crops are a throwback to the early days of synthetic pesticides, when farmers were encouraged to spray even if their crops didn't appear to need it. The Bt crops show a similar lack of discrimination: they are programmed to churn out toxin during the entire growing season, regardless of the level of infestation. This sort of prophylactic control greatly increases the likelihood of resistance because it tends to maximize exposure to the toxin—it's the plant equivalent of treating antibiotics like vitamins. . . .

The Weeds

The global transgenic harvest is currently dominated, not by Bt crops, but by herbicide-resistant crops (HRCs), which occupy 20 million hectares worldwide. HRCs are sold as part of a "technology package" comprised of HRC seed and the herbicide the crop is designed to resist. The two principal product lines are currently Monsanto's "Roundup Ready" crops—so-named because they tolerate Monsanto's best-selling herbicide, "Roundup" (glyphosate)—and AgrEvo's "Liberty Link" crops, which tolerate that company's "Liberty" herbicide (glufosinate). . . .

The bigger problem is that HRCs, like Bt crops, are really just an extension of the current pesticide paradigm. HRCs may permit a reduction in herbicide use over the short term, but obviously their widespread adoption would encourage herbicide dependency. In many parts of the developing world, where herbicides are not now common, the herbicide habit could mean substantial additional environmental stresses: herbicides are toxic to many soil organisms, they can pollute groundwater, and they may have long-term effects on both people and wildlife. . . .

As with the Bt crops, the early promise of HRCs is liable to be undercut by the very mentality that inspired them: the single-minded chemical pursuit of the pest. . . .

Toward a New Feudalism

The advent of transgenic crops raises serious social questions as well—beginning with ownership. All transgenic seed is patented, as are most nontransgenic commercial varieties. But beginning in the 1980s, the tendency in industrialized countries and in international law has been to permit increasingly broad agricultural patents—and not just on varieties but even on specific genes. Under the earlier, more limited patents, farmers could buy seed and use it in their own breeding; they could grow it out and save some of the resulting seed for the next year; they could even trade it for other seed. About the only thing they couldn't do was sell it outright. But under the broader patents, all of those activities are illegal; the purchaser is essentially just paying for one-time use of the germplasm. . . .

Patents and similar legal mechanisms may be giving companies additional control over farmers. As a way of securing their patent rights, biotech companies are requiring farmers to sign "seed contracts" when they purchase transgenic seed—a wholly new phenomenon in agriculture. The contracts may stipulate what brand of pesticides the farmer must use on the crop—a kind of legal cement for those crop-herbicide "technology packages." And the contracts generally forbid the types of activities that had been permitted under the earlier patent regimes. . . .

A recent invention—officially entitled the "gene protection technology" but popularly dubbed the "terminator technology"—may make the seed contracts a biological reality. The terminator prevents harvested seeds from germinating. Its principal inventor, a U.S. Department of Agriculture molecular biologist named Melvin Oliver, notes that "the technology primarily targets Second and Third World markets"—in effect guaranteeing patent rights even in nations where patent enforcement is weak or non-existent. The terminator may also encourage the patenting of some major crops, such as rice, wheat, and sorghum, that have generally been ignored by private-sector breeders. Although there has been a great deal of public sector development of these crops, it has been difficult for private companies to make money on them, because it is relatively easy for farmers to breed stable, productive varieties on their own. The terminator could allow companies to get a better "grip" on such crops. . . .

But beyond these control issues, there remains the basic question of biotech's potential for feeding the world's billions. Here too, the current trends are not very encouraging. At present, the industry has funneled its immense pool of investment into a limited range of products for which there are large, secured markets within the capital-intensive production systems of the First World. There is very little connection between that kind of research and the lives of the world's hungry. HRCs, for example, are not helpful to poor farmers who rely on manual labor to pull weeds because they couldn't possibly afford herbicides. (The immediate opportunities for biotech in the developing world are not the subsistence farmers, of course, but the larger operations, which are often producing for export rather than for local consumption.)

Just to get a sense of proportion on this subject, consider this comparison. The entire annual budget of the Consultative Group for International Agricultural Research (CGIAR), a consortium of international research centers that form the world's largest public-sector crop breeding effort, amounts to $400 million. The amount that Monsanto spent to develop Roundup Ready soybeans alone is estimated at $500 million.

In such numbers, one can see a kind of financial disconnect. Per Pinstrup-Andersen, director of the International Food Policy Research Institute, the CGIAR's policy arm, puts it flatly: "the private sector will not develop crops to solve poor people's problems, because there is not enough money in it." The very nature of their affliction—poverty—makes hungry people poor customers for expensive technologies.

In addition to the financial obstacle, there is a biological obstacle that may limit the role of biotech as agricultural savior. The crop traits that would be most useful to subsistence farmers tend to be very complex. Miguel Altieri, an entomologist at the University of California at Berkeley, identifies the kind of products that would make sense in a subsistence context: "crop varieties responsive to low levels of soil fertility, crops tolerant of saline or drought conditions and other stresses of marginal lands, improved varieties that are not dependent on agro-chemical inputs for increased yields, varieties that are compatible with small, diverse, capital-poor farm settings." In HRCs and Bt crops, the engineering involves the insertion of a single gene. Most of the traits Altieri is talking about are probably governed by many genes, and for the present at least, that kind of complexity is far beyond the technology's reach. . . .

Beyond the Techno-Fix

On a 300-acre farm in Boone, Iowa—the heart of the U.S. corn belt—Dick Thompson rotates corn, soybeans, oats, wheat interplanted with clover, and a hay combination that includes an assortment of grasses and legumes. The pests that plague neighboring farmers—including the corn borer targeted by Bt corn—are generally a minor part of the picture on Thompson's farm. High crop diversity tends to reduce insect populations because insect pests are usually "specialists" on one particular crop. In a very diverse setting, no single pest is likely to be able to get the upper hand. Diversity also tends to shut out weeds, because complex cropping uses resources more efficiently than monocultures, so there's less left over for the weeds to consume. Thompson also keeps the weeds down by grazing a herd of cattle—a rarity on midwestern corn farms. Even without herbicides, Thompson's farm has been on conservation tillage for the last three decades. The cattle, a hog operation, and the nitrogen-fixing legumes provide the soil nutrients that most U.S. farmers buy in a bag. The soil organic matter content—the sentinel indicator of soil health—registers at 6 percent on Thompson's land, which is more than twice that of his neighbors. (Untouched Midwestern prairie registers at 7 percent.) Thompson's soybean and corn yields are well above the county average and even as the U.S. government continues to bail out indebted farmers, Thompson is making money. He profits both from his healthy soil and crops, and from the fact that his "input" costs—for chemical fertilizer, pesticides, and so forth—are almost nil.

In the activities of people like . . . Thompson it is possible to see a very different kind of agricultural paradigm, which could move farming beyond the techno-fix approach that currently prevails. Known as agroecology, this paradigm recognizes the farm as an ecosystem—an agroecosystem—and employs ecological principles to improve productivity and build stability. The emphasis is on adapting farm design and practice to the ecological processes actually occurring in the fields and in the landscape that surrounds them. Agroecology aims to substitute detailed (and usually local) ecological knowledge for off-the-shelf and off-the-farm "magic bullet" solutions. The point is to treat the disease, rather than just the symptoms. Instead of engineering a corn variety that is toxic to corn rootworm, for example, an agroecologist would ask why there's a rootworm problem in the first place. . . .

There is no question that biotech contains some real potential for agriculture, for instance as a supplement to conventional breeding or as a means of studying crop pathogens. But if the industry continues to follow its current trajectory, then biotech's likely contribution will be marginal at best and at worst, given the additional dimensions of ecological and social unpredictability—who knows? In any case, the biggest hope for agriculture is not something biochemists are going to find in a test tube. The biggest opportunities will be found in what farmers already know, or in what they can readily discover on their farms.

Periodical Bibliography

The following articles have been selected to supplement the diverse views presented in this chapter. Addresses are provided for periodicals not indexed in the *Readers' Guide to Periodical Literature*, the *Alternative Press Index*, the *Social Sciences Index*, or the *Index to Legal Periodicals and Books*.

John Carey	"Are Bio-Foods Safe?" *Business Week*, December 20, 1999.
CQ Researcher	"Food Safety Battle: Organic vs. Biotech," September 4, 1998.
Greg Dicum	"It Isn't Easy Being Green," *New York Times Magazine*, August 22, 1999.
Gregg Easterbrook	"Food for the Future," *New York Times*, November 19, 1999.
Issues and Controversies On File	"Genetically Engineered Food," February 12, 1999.
Jeffrey Kluger	"Food Fight," *Time*, September 13, 1999.
Phillip Longman	"The Curse of Frankenfood," *U.S. News & World Report*, July 26, 1999.
James P. Lucier	"Freezing Out the Farmers," *Insight on the News*, November 15, 1999.
John R. Luoma	"Pandora's Pantry," *Mother Jones*, January/February 2000.
Charles C. Mann	"Biotech Goes Wild," *Technology Review*, July/August 1999.
Maria Margaronis	"The Politics of Food," *Nation*, December 27, 1999.
Mark Nichols	"Tampering with the Natural Order," *Maclean's*, May 17, 1999.
Robert W. Reynolds	"Agricultural Biotechnology: Opportunities and Risks," *USA Today*, July 1999.
Peter Rosset	"Why Genetically Altered Food Won't Conquer Hunger," *New York Times*, September 1, 1999.

CHAPTER 4

How Should Genetic Engineering Be Regulated?

Chapter Preface

One of the most contentious issues regarding the regulation of genetic research involves the use of stem cells derived from human embryos. As mammalian embryos develop, their cells become genetically programmed to become a specific type of tissue—heart, nerve, skin, etc. Embryonic stem cells are special because they can be genetically manipulated into becoming any type of tissue. This makes them ideal for gene therapy and a host of other medical applications. Scientists with a supply of stem cells might be able to, for example, genetically engineer the cells in the lab, then induce them to become bone marrow cells or livers for patients in need of transplants.

The problem with stem cells is their source: Until recently, researchers could only obtain stem cells from aborted fetuses or from human embryos created through the process of in vitro fertilization (IVF). Thus this type of research was intertwined with the abortion debate and hindered by a ban on federal funding for experiments involving aborted fetuses and most IVF embryos.

However, scientists' hopes for learning more about stem cells were renewed in February 1997, when Ian Wilmut announced that he had cloned a sheep named Dolly. "Essentially," writes science writer Gregg Easterbrook, "he did this by taking cells from an adult lamb [and] making them act like stem cells. . . . Researchers are now finding indications that small amounts of stem cells continue to exist, overlooked, in the adult's nerve tissue and elsewhere."

Inspired by this advance, scientists are pressing the National Institutes of Health to increase funding for research on stem cells taken from adult tissues and human umbilical cords rather than from human embryos. While many pro-life groups would accept this type of research, they are alarmed by scientists who want to completely lift the ban on human embryo research.

The debate over the regulation of stem cell research is complex and constantly changing as new experiments, such as the cloning of Dolly, change people's view of what is scientifically possible. The authors in the following chapter offer other arguments for how genetic engineering should or should not be regulated.

> *"We have established ethics committees and protocols for reviewing the impact of scientific and technological innovations. . . . Yet our reactions remain largely uncoordinated and not deeply reflective or productive."*

Genetic Engineering Should Be More Closely Regulated

Jane Maienschein

In the following viewpoint, Jane Maienschein, a professor of philosophy and biology at Arizona State University, argues that society should more closely examine the ethical, legal, and social implications of advances in genetic engineering. However, she notes that regulation of genetic engineering will be difficult because, much more so than with other technologies, people's views about genetic engineering are closely tied to their most fundamental values. She maintains that society's conflicting views about genetic engineering—as either "just another technology" or as unethical meddling with nature—must be resolved before choices can be made about how the new technologies should or should not be used.

As you read, consider the following questions:

1. What explanation does the author offer for why Europeans are more concerned than Americans about genetically engineered food?
2. How did scientists respond to the first cases of DNA manipulation in the 1970s, according to Maienschein?
3. What type of program did James Watson institute as first director of the Human Genome Project, according to the author?

Excerpted from Jane Maienschein, "Who's in Charge of the Gene Genie?" *The World & I*, January 2000. Copyright ©2000 *The World & I*, a publication of The Washington Times Corporation. Reprinted with permission from *The World & I*.

Americans have always cheered the advances of engineering, saying that engineering is good, that building better bridges, housing, airplanes, computers, water and sewage systems, transportation systems, and on and on are all good. Replacing injured arms or legs, diseased kidneys, and hearts—these are also good, as is producing more abundant food and water. Developing countries look to the United States for technological leadership, and our advances seem to offer all the medical, agricultural, and economic success that people everywhere want. So what's the problem? All these existing and accepted technologies involve "playing God" in the sense of using human initiatives to make life better for those who are injured, malnourished, or whatever. Is genetic engineering really any different?

The Case of Genetically Modified Food

European consumers have recently expressed their fears about foods genetically modified with foreign genes spliced into otherwise normal food products. One of these, the Bt gene, taken from a bacterium, codes for a molecule that is toxic to insect pests of such food crops as potatoes and corn. European consumers are worried about their own personal health and also the unpredictable effects on the environment. They do not trust large companies that stand to profit, nor the scientists who work there, when they offer assurances that this is all tested and "safe." These consumers, and the market that reflects their opinions, have one answer: Yes, genetic engineering is different, because it has the potential not only to disrupt and genetically alter our environment but change our very biological selves. . . .

The ability to splice genetic sequences into living organisms where they would not normally be found raises fears that we are somehow creating Frankenstein-like versions of corn or unleashing something that we will not be able to control. This is what bothers people, suggesting that we are crossing some natural boundary that has protected us in the past. Certainly it is wise and sensible to ask about whether and where such boundaries might exist. But to know that we have reached such a special boundary we need a clear argument about what is different. We have fears and concerns, but these are not grounded in compelling logic or clear reasoning. Why should genetically modified foods raise special questions when medical procedures do not?

Cultural Differences

Here we come to questions about the relevant constituencies. In Europe, much more than in the United States, there is a strong "green" orientation, and "the environment" becomes a constituent with legitimate legal and social interests to be protected. For "green" Europeans, the environment is taken as something natural, and as much as possible undisturbed by human interventions, and advocates for the environment lobby against human actions that can threaten what is natural. For them, genetic modification of crops is unnatural and hence to be rejected. We should not arrogate unto ourselves the power to change and disturb what is natural, the reasoning goes, for we are instead intended to exercise stewardship over other species and natural surroundings.

Historians and sociologists suggest that the relative lack of a natural environment in Europe leads to a heightened awareness and concern about protecting nature there. Americans, by contrast, have not so widely or so militantly adopted such an environmentalist view, perhaps because we have so much apparent wilderness that we feel buffered from assaults on what is natural. Nature abounds, after all—in our national parks, our forests, and even our backyards as deer and coyotes expand their territories into suburban neighborhoods. Looking beyond Europe and the United States, we see that in the poor countries the scramble to survive seems to preclude investments of time or energy in efforts to save "nature."

Who Is Right?

Given the differences between Europe and the United States, who is right? It does matter, after all, since economic markets are affected by value judgments and resulting regulations concerning what is allowed. If the European or Japanese markets will not accept genetically modified foods, then it might be more profitable not to grow them. But GM foods can be cheaper and more productive, requiring fewer pesticides and less physical intervention during the growing process, which is at least an obvious short-term advantage. Thus, the larger market forces and values that affect them do matter. If the market is the judge, then it looks as though those opposing GM foods may be "right." It remains to be seen whether the fears of environmental damage are real, however.

Genetic Engineering of Humans Should Be Limited to the Treatment of Disease

Society faces a real danger. In the name of minor "improvements" that we see as conveniences, we might start using human genetic engineering to attempt to change ourselves and then our children. Engineering the human germ line would result in permanent changes in the gene pool. We as a society have yet to end discrimination, including its most virulent expression, ethnic cleansing. What would happen if we add intentional genetic enhancement to the mix? . . .

Our only protection is to accept clear stopping points. And the only way to achieve those is to make sure that society is informed and can recognize the dangers and prevent misuses before it is too late. If such crucial decisions are left to the marketplace, might we ultimately engineer ourselves to the point where we are no longer human beings? . . . Our duty is to go into the era of human genetic engineering as respectfully as possible. That means that we should not use human genetic engineering for any other purpose than the treatment of serious disease, no matter how tempting it might be.

W. French Anderson, *U.S. News & World Report*, January 1, 2000.

What about genetically modified animals? We now have mice with augmented "smart genes" that make them apparently more intelligent—in the sense of being able to perform particular defined tasks more successfully. The joke about why anybody would want smarter mice notwithstanding, this is real, and it is being done. There has been no outpouring of negative opinion or concern. Rather, the media have reported the results with enthusiasm and sometimes breathless wonder at how long it will be before we can do the same in humans.

What about genetically modified humans? Opinion polls show that Americans are enthusiastic about the prospects for curing cancer or whatever disease, with breakthrough discoveries that research funded by the National Institutes of Health (NIH) will bring us—well, just any day now. If only we invest enough in mission- and disease-oriented research, popular opinion seems to say, we can solve the problems. We can create wonderful babies for otherwise infertile couples by removing eggs and sperm and combining them. Along the way, at some point in the future, we will presumably have techniques to make better humans. In principle, we should be able to engineer the genetic composition of each individual, and therefore the population, by selecting only those genes and then those individuals that we want to have live and eliminating the rest—through fetal surgery, selective implantation, or targeted abortion. While the discussion usually centers on the medical procedures, these manipulations are also fundamentally about genetic engineering. There are choices of which genes and which combinations of genes (which individuals) to allow to live.

Competing Values

Astonishingly, this work is largely unregulated. Most occurs in fertility clinics, and Congress has left the clinics to develop their own value systems and to make their own assumptions. The best have clear guidelines and protocols that they follow carefully, while the worst, as in any industry, are sloppy and careless. Our take-home point here is that the practices in these clinics are based on different values.

The clinic that chooses to increase the chances of a pregnancy by fertilizing many eggs and then implanting them all in the mother exhibits little concern for the possibility all the eggs will die because the mother cannot carry them to term. This clinic also shows little concern for the possibility that if the mother does carry all the eggs to term, as has happened recently with seven and then eight births, it will be at great medical cost—and someone will have to pay that cost. By contrast, the clinic that fertilizes and implants only a small number—and perhaps chooses those that have the "best genes"—acts more responsibly by accepting the risk of lower pregnancy rates and disappointed clients, but avoiding the heartbreak of miscarriages and problems of multiple fetuses. The values guiding these decisions are social, ethical, political, and economic—not scientific. The ways of going about knowing what is possible and judging what is right begin with a variety of competing underlying values and assumptions about what matters and what counts as evidence in favor of any given claim. At the root, we have different and competing epistemologies.

What follows from this recognition that life is messy and full of conflicting values and competing epistemologies? Surely we knew that already? Yes, of course, but did we face what it means to accept this? It means that we cannot turn to just one source as the ultimate authority, whether the church (and there are, after all, many competing alternatives even here, or even competing interpretations of the Christian Bible), the king (since very few of us have one anymore anyway), the Congress or Parliament or other ruling group (since increasingly few of us vote or respect our elected representatives anyway, according to polls in many countries), or any one expert (and who is an expert anyway?). It cannot be the scientist-as-expert who will decide how to use genetic engineering, even though it is scientists who must tell us what is possible and how the technology works.

Learning from Experience

The reaction to those first cases of recombining DNA in the 1970s is instructive. The scientists themselves quickly saw that applying the techniques could lead to the irreversible creation of "unnatural" genetic "monsters." They did not anticipate disaster, but they called for careful consideration of what they knew and what values should guide application of the knowledge. They organized a special meeting in Asilomar, California, in 1975 to consider the scientific realities, the prospects, and the implications of genetic recombination. After intense discussion with lawyers and members of the press, they issued a statement. They called for a moratorium on certain kinds of research thought to carry the greatest risks until we gained further knowledge, and some of them worked with the NIH to develop a set of guidelines.

Learning from experience since then, we have established ethics committees and protocols for reviewing the impact of scientific and technological innovations. A set of physical and biological protections has been put in place for particular kinds of genetic engineering research carried out with public funding. And when new technologies arise, we appeal to ethics advisory committees. James Watson, as first director of the Human Genome Project, thought it politically expedient to develop a program to explore the ethical, legal, and social implications of genetic discoveries.

Yet our reactions remain largely uncoordinated and not deeply reflective or productive. In the face of new advances such as cloning or genetic modification of foods, Congress typically fusses around and calls hearings. But we have no acknowledged leaders or procedures for resolving conflicts between competing systems of values and epistemologies.

The Need for Intelligent Social Discussion

Values beyond scientists' desire to pursue knowledge at all costs should influence our social choices concerning how to use technologies like genetic engineering. Yet the fearful Luddites who oppose all innovation should not prevail without clear reason. We need intelligent social discussion of the competing values, as well as intelligent and reflective social negotiation across differences. Not everything is equally good, but we have no way of knowing that one particular set of values ought to prevail. The decisions are a matter of social convention and negotiation, but we have not yet established the rules to guide this negotiation. Senator Edward Kennedy was right in saying [in 1976] that "the real problem is to understand the social consequences of what science can now enable us to do." We just don't know how to do that.

"Never postpone experiments that have clearly defined future benefits for fear of dangers that can't be quantified."

Genetic Engineering Should Not Be More Closely Regulated

James D. Watson

In the following viewpoint, James D. Watson argues that restrictions should not be placed on genetic research. In his view, the impetus behind such regulations is usually an irrational fear of new technology. These fears are not an adequate basis for banning or postponing potentially beneficial experiments, he asserts. Watson discusses the fear that the first recombinant-DNA experiments sparked in the early 1970s, and compares it to the current reluctance among governments to permit the genetic manipulation of human sperm and egg cells. In 1953 James Watson, along with Francis Crick, won a Noble Prize for their discovery of the double helical structure of DNA. Watson was the first director of the Human Genome Project and is now president of Cold Spring Harbor Laboratory.

As you read, consider the following questions:
1. What evidence does the author provide to support his view that "recombinant-DNA may rank as the safest revolutionary technology ever developed"?
2. In Watson's opinion, why have governments been reluctant to permit the genetic engineering of human germ cells?
3. In the author's view, what will be the purpose of the first germ-line genetic manipulation of humans?

Reprinted from James D. Watson, "All for the Good," *Time*, January 11, 1999. Reprinted with permission from Time-Life Syndications.

There is lots of zip in DNA-based biology today. With each passing year it incorporates an ever increasing fraction of the life sciences, ranging from single-cell organisms, like bacteria and yeast, to the complexities of the human brain. All this wonderful biological frenzy was unimaginable when I first entered the world of genetics. In 1948, biology was an all too descriptive discipline near the bottom of science's totem pole, with physics at its top. By then Einstein's turn-of-the-century ideas about the interconversion of matter and energy had been transformed into the powers of the atom. If not held in check, the weapons they made possible might well destroy the very fabric of civilized human life. So physicists of the late 1940s were simultaneously revered for making atoms relevant to society and feared for what their toys could do if they were to fall into the hands of evil.

Such ambivalent feelings are now widely held toward biology. The double-helical structure of DNA, initially admired for its intellectual simplicity, today represents to many a double-edged sword that can be used for evil as well as good. No sooner had scientists at Stanford University in 1973 begun rearranging DNA molecules in test tubes (and, equally important, reinserting the novel DNA segments back into living cells) than critics began likening these "recombinant" DNA procedures to the physicist's power to break apart atoms. Might not some of the test-tube-rearranged DNA molecules impart to their host cells disease-causing capacities that, like nuclear weapons, are capable of seriously disrupting human civilization? Soon there were cries from both scientists and nonscientists that such research might best be ruled by stringent regulations—if not laws.

As a result, several years were to pass before the full power of recombinant-DNA technology got into the hands of working scientists, who by then were itching to explore previously unattainable secrets of life. Happily, the proposals to control recombinant-DNA research through legislation never got close to enactment. And when anti-DNA doomsday scenarios failed to materialize, even the modestly restrictive governmental regulations began to wither away. In retrospect, recombinant-DNA may rank as the safest revolutionary technology ever developed. To my knowledge, not one fatality, much less illness, has been caused by a genetically manipulated organism.

The moral I draw from this painful episode is this: Never postpone experiments that have clearly defined future benefits for fear of dangers that can't be quantified. Though it may sound at first uncaring, we can react rationally only to real (as opposed to hypothetical) risks. Yet for several years we postponed important experiments on the genetic basis of cancer, for example, because we took much too seriously spurious arguments that the genes at the root of human cancer might themselves be dangerous to work with.

Government Regulation of Genetic Engineering Could Lead to Government Control

[Leon] Kass does have a point . . . when he writes in *Commentary*, "Even people who might otherwise welcome the growth of genetic knowledge and technology are worried about the coming power of geneticists, genetic engineers, and, in particular, governmental authorities armed with genetic technology."

There is a threat of government control. Some intellectuals are already succumbing to the temptation of government-supported and mandated eugenics, lest the benefits of genetic engineering be spread unequally. "Laissez-faire eugenics will emerge from the free choices of millions of parents," warns *Time* magazine columnist Robert Wright. He then concludes, "The only way to avoid Huxleyesque social stratification may be for government to get into the eugenics business."

Clearly we must be on guard against any attempts to harness this new technology to government-mandated ends. But a Brave New World of government eugenics is not an inevitable consequence of biomedical progress. It depends instead on whether we leave individuals free to make decisions about their biological futures or whether, in the name of equality or of control, we give that power to centralized bureaucracies. Huxley's world had no "laissez-faire eugenics" emerging from free choice; *Brave New World* is about a centrally planned society.

Ronald Bailey, *Reason*, December 1999.

Though most forms of DNA manipulation are now effectively unregulated, one important potential goal remains blocked. Experiments aimed at learning how to insert functional genetic material into human germ cells—sperm and eggs—remain off limits to most of the world's scientists. No governmental body wants to take responsibility for initiating steps that might help redirect the course of future human evolution. These decisions reflect widespread concerns that we, as humans, may not have the wisdom to modify the most precious of all human treasures—our chromosomal "instruction books." Dare we be entrusted with improving upon the results of the several million years of Darwinian natural selection? Are human germ cells Rubicons that geneticists may never cross?

Unlike many of my peers, I'm reluctant to accept such reasoning, again using the argument that you should never put off doing something useful for fear of evil that may never arrive. The first germ-line gene manipulations are unlikely to be attempted for frivolous reasons. Nor does the state of today's science provide the knowledge that would be needed to generate "superpersons" whose far-ranging talents would make those who are genetically unmodified feel redundant and unwanted. Such creations will remain denizens of science fiction, not the real world, far into the future. When they are finally attempted, germ-line genetic manipulations will probably be done to change a death sentence into a life verdict—by creating children who are resistant to a deadly virus, for example, much the way we can already protect plants from viruses by inserting antiviral DNA segments into their genomes.

If appropriate go-ahead signals come, the first resulting gene-bettered children will in no sense threaten human civilization. They will be seen as special only by those in their immediate circles, and are likely to pass as unnoticed in later life as the now grownup "test-tube baby" Louise Brown does today. If they grow up healthily gene-bettered, more such children will follow, and they and those whose lives are enriched by their existence will rejoice that science has again improved human life. If, however, the added genetic material fails to work, better procedures must be developed before more couples commit their psyches toward such inherently unsettling pathways to producing healthy children.

Moving forward will not be for the faint of heart. But if the new century witnesses failure, let it be because our science is not yet up to the job, not because we don't have the courage to make less random the sometimes most unfair courses of human evolution.

"Corporations are assuming ownership and control over the hereditary blueprints of life itself."

Scientists Should Not Be Allowed to Patent Genes

Jeremy Rifkin

Jeremy Rifkin is president of the Foundation on Economic Trends and the author of *The Biotech Century: Harnessing the Gene and Remaking the World*, from which the following viewpoint is excerpted. In it, he warns that research universities and biotechnology companies are being allowed to patent the genes they discover in the course of their research. Rifkin believes that genes are products of nature, and thus should not be given the same legal recognition as man-made inventions. He concludes that the race to claim ownership of human, plant, and animal genes will give biotechnology corporations enormous power over the future of genetic engineering.

As you read, consider the following questions:
1. According to Rifkin, why did the U.S. Patents and Trademark Office (PTO) initially reject Ananda Chakrabarty's application for a patent on a genetically engineered microorganism, and on what basis did the Supreme Court overrule the PTO?
2. What agreement does the author compare to "the European settlers giving the American Indians trinkets in return for the island of Manhattan"?

While the 20th century was shaped by breakthroughs in physics and chemistry, the 21st century will belong to the biological sciences. Scientists are deciphering the genetic code, unlocking the mystery of millions of years of evolution. Global life science companies, in turn, are beginning to exploit these new advances. The raw resources of the new economic epoch are genes—already being used in businesses ranging from agriculture and bio-remediation to energy and pharmaceuticals.

By 2025, we may be living in a world remade by a revolution unmatched in history. The biotech revolution raises unprecedented ethical questions we've barely begun to discuss. Will the artificial creation of cloned and transgenic animals mean the end of nature and the substitution of a bio-industrial world? Will the release of genetically engineered life forms into the biosphere cause catastrophic genetic pollution? What will it mean to live in a world where babies are customized in the womb—and where people are stereotyped and discriminated against on the basis of their genotype? What risks do we take in attempting to design more "perfect" human beings?

Should We Patent Life?

At the heart of this new commercial revolution is a chilling question of great ethical impact, whose resolution will affect civilization for centuries to come: *Should we patent life?* The practice has already gotten a green light, through a controversial Supreme Court decision and a subsequent ruling by the Patent and Trademark Office in the 1980s. But if the question were put directly to the American people, would they agree? If you alter one gene in a chimpanzee, does that make the animal a human "invention"? If you isolate the gene for breast cancer, does that give you the right to "own" it? Should a handful of global corporations be allowed to patent all human genes?

On the eve of the biotech century, we do still have an opportunity to raise ethical issues like these—although the window is rapidly closing.

We've only completed the first decade of a revolution that may span several centuries. But already there are 1,400 biotech companies in the U.S., with a total of nearly $13 billion in annual revenues and more than 100,000 employees. Development is proceeding in an astonishing number of areas:

At Harvard University, scientists have grown human bladders and kidneys in laboratory jars. Monsanto hopes to have a plastic-producing plant on the market by the year 2003—following up on the work of Chris Sommerville at the Carnegie Institution of Washington, who inserted a plastic-making gene into a mustard plant. Another biotech company, the Institute of Genomic Research, has successfully sequenced a microbe that can absorb large amounts of radioactivity and be used to dispose of deadly radioactive waste. The first genetically engineered insect, a predator mite, was released in 1996 by researchers at the University of Florida, who hope it will eat other mites that damage strawberries and similar crops.

At the University of Wisconsin, scientists have genetically altered brooding turkey hens to increase their productivity, by eliminating the "brooding" instinct: the desire to sit on and hatch eggs. Other researchers are experimenting with the creation of sterile salmon who will not have the suicidal urge to spawn, but will remain in the open sea, to be commercially harvested. Michigan State University scientists say that by breaking the spawning cycle of chinook salmon, they can produce seventy-pound salmon, compared to less than eighteen pounds for a fish returning to spawn. In short, the mothering instinct and the mating instinct are being bred out of animals.

With genetic engineering, humanity is extending its reach over the forces of nature far beyond the scope of any previous technology—with the possible exception of the nuclear bomb. At the same time, corporations are assuming ownership and control over the hereditary blueprints of life itself. Can any reasonable person believe such power is without risk?

The Legal Background

Genes are the "green gold" of the biotech century, and companies that control them will exercise tremendous power over the world economy. Multinational corporations are already scouting the continents in search of this new precious resource, hoping to locate microbes, plants, animals, and humans with rare genetic traits that might have future market potential. Having located the desired traits, biotech companies are modifying them and seeking patent protection for their new "inventions."

The worldwide race to patent the gene pool is the culmination of a 500-year odyssey to enclose the ecosystems of the Earth. That journey began in feudal England in the 1500s, with the passage of the great "enclosure acts," which privatized the village commons—transforming the land from a community trust to private real estate. Today, virtually every square foot of landmass on the planet is under private ownership or government control.

But enclosure of the land was just the beginning. Today, the ocean's coastal waters are commercially leased, the air has been converted into commercial airline corridors, and even the electromagnetic spectrum is considered commercial property—leased for use by radio, TV, and telephone companies. Now the most intimate commons of all—the gene pool—is being enclosed and reduced to private commercial property.

The enclosure of the genetic commons began in 1971, when an Indian microbiologist and General Electric employee, Ananda Chakrabarty, applied to the U.S. Patents and Trademark Office (PTO) for a patent on a genetically engineered microorganism designed to consume oil spills. The PTO rejected the request, arguing that living things are not patentable. The case was appealed all the way to the Supreme Court, which in 1980—by a slim margin of five to four—ruled in favor of Chakrabarty. Speaking for the majority, Chief Justice Warren Burger argued that "the relevant distinction was not between living and inanimate things," but whether or not Chakrabarty's microbe was a "human-made invention."

In the aftermath of that historic decision, bioengineering technology shed its pristine academic garb and bounded into the marketplace. On October 13, 1980—just months after the court's ruling—Genentech publicly offered one million shares of stock at $35 per share. By the time the trading bell had rung that first day, the stock was selling at over $500 per share. And Genentech had yet to introduce a single product.

Chemical, pharmaceutical, agribusiness, and biotech startups everywhere sped up their research—mindful that the granting of patent protection meant the possibility of harnessing the genetic commons for vast commercial gain. Some observers, however, were not so enthused. Ethicist Leon Kass asked:

> What is the principled limit to this beginning extension of the domain of private ownership and dominion over living nature . . . ? The principle used in Chakrabarty says that there is nothing in the nature of a being, not even in the patentor himself, that makes him immune to being patented.

While the Supreme Court decision lent an air of legal legitimacy to the emerging biotech industry, a Patent Office decision in 1987 opened the floodgates. In a complete about-face, the PTO ruled that all genetically engineered multicellular living organisms—including animals—are potentially patentable. The Commissioner of Patents and Trademarks at the time, Donald J. Quigg, attempted to calm a shocked public by asserting that the decision covered every creature except human beings—because the Thirteenth Amendment to the Constitution forbids human slavery. On the other hand, human embryos and fetuses as well as human genes, tissues, and organs were now potentially patentable.

Suspect Rulings

What makes the Supreme Court decision and Patent Office ruling suspect, from a legal point of view, is that they defy previous patent rulings that say one cannot claim a "discovery of nature" as an invention. No one would suggest that scientists who isolated, classified, and described the properties of chemical elements in the periodic table—such as oxygen and helium—ought to be granted a patent on them. Yet someone who isolates and classifies the properties of human genes can patent them.

The European Patent Office, for example, awarded a patent to the U.S. company Biocyte, giving it ownership of all human blood cells which have come from the umbilical cord of a newborn child and are being used for any therapeutic purposes. The patent is so broad that it allows this one company to refuse the use of any blood cells from the umbilical cord to any individual unwilling to pay the patent fee. Blood cells from the umbilical cord are particularly important for marrow transplants, making it a valuable commercial asset. It should be emphasized that this patent was awarded simply because Biocyte was able to isolate the blood cells and deep-freeze them. The company made no change in the blood itself.

A similarly broad patent was awarded to Systemix Inc. of Palo Alto, California, by the U.S. Patent Office, covering all human bone marrow stem cells. This extraordinary patent on a human body part was awarded despite the fact that Systemix had done nothing whatsoever to alter or engineer the cells. Dr. Peter Quisenberry, the medical affairs vice chairman of the Leukemia Society of America, quipped, "Where do you draw the line? Can you patent a hand?"

The Race to Patent Life

The life patents race is gearing up in the wake of government and commercial efforts to map the approximately 100,000 human genes that make up the human genome—a project with enormous commercial potential. As soon as a gene is tagged its "discoverer" is likely to apply for a patent, often before knowing the function of the gene. In 1991, J. Craig Venter, then head of the National Institute of Health Genome Mapping Research Team, resigned his government post to head up a genomics company funded with more than $70 million in venture capital. At the same time, Venter and his colleagues filed for patents on more than 2,000 human brain genes. Many researchers on the Human Genome Project were shocked and angry, charging Venter with attempting to profit off research paid for by American taxpayers.

Nobel laureate James Watson, co-discoverer of the DNA double helix, called the Venter patent claims "sheer lunacy." Still, it's likely that within less than ten years, all 100,000 or so genes that comprise the genetic legacy of our species will be patented—making them the exclusive intellectual property of global corporations.

The patenting of life is creating a firestorm of controversy.

Several years ago, an Alaskan businessman named John Moore found his own body parts had been patented, without his knowledge, by the University of California at Los Angeles (UCLA), and licensed to the Sandoz Pharmaceutical Corp. Moore had been diagnosed with a rare cancer and underwent treatment at UCLA. A researcher there discovered that Moore's spleen tissue produced a blood protein that facilitates the growth of white blood cells valuable as anti-cancer agents. The university created a cell line from Moore's spleen tissue and obtained a patent on the "invention." The cell line is estimated to be worth more than $3 billion.

Reprinted with permission from Axel Scheffler.

Moore subsequently sued, claiming a property right over his own tissue. But in 1990, the California Supreme Court ruled against him, saying Moore had no such ownership right. Human body parts, the court argued, could not be bartered as a commodity in the marketplace.

The irony of the decision was captured by judge Broussard, in his dissenting opinion. The ruling "does *not* mean that body parts may not be bought or sold," he wrote. "[T]he majority's holding simply bars *plaintiff*, the source of the cells, from obtaining the benefit of the cell's value, but permits *defendants*, who allegedly obtained the cells from plaintiff by improper means, to retain and exploit the full economic value of their ill-gotten gains."

North vs. South

A battle of historic proportions has also emerged between the high-technology nations of the North and the developing nations of the South, over ownership of the planet's genetic treasures. Some Third World leaders say the North is attempting to seize the biological commons, most of which is in the rich tropical regions of the Southern Hemisphere, and that their nations should be compensated for use of genetic resources. Corporate and governmental leaders in the North maintain that the genes increase in value only when manipulated using sophisticated gene-splicing techniques, so there's no obligation to compensate the South.

To ease growing tensions, a number of companies have proposed sharing a portion of their gains. Merck & Co., the pharmaceutical giant (often considered a leader in social responsibility), entered into an agreement recently with a research organization in Costa Rica, the National Biodiversity Institute, to pay the organization a paltry $1 million to secure the group's plant, microorganism, and insect samples. Critics liken the deal to European settlers giving American Indians trinkets in return for the island of Manhattan. The recipient organization, on the other hand, is granting a right to bio-prospect on land it has no historic claim to in the first place—while indigenous peoples are locked out of the agreement.

Such agreements are beginning to meet with resistance from countries and non-governmental organizations (NGOs) in the Southern Hemisphere. They claim that what Northern companies are calling "discoveries" are really the pirating of the indigenous knowledge of native peoples and cultures. To defuse opposition, biotech corporations are seeking to impose a uniform intellectual property regime worldwide. And they've gone a long way toward achieving that with the passage of the Trade Related Aspects of Intellectual Property Agreements (TRIPS) at the Uruguay Round of the General Agreement on Tariffs and Trade (GATT). Sculpted by companies like Bristol Myers, Merck, Pfizer, Dupont, and Monsanto, the TRIPS agreement makes no allowance for indigenous knowledge, and grants companies free access to genetic material from around the world.

Suman Sahai, director of the Gene Campaign—an NGO in New Delhi—makes the point, "God didn't give us 'rice' or 'wheat' or 'potato.'" These were once wild plants that were domesticated over eons of time and patiently bred by generations of farmers. Sahai asks, "Who did all of that work?" Groups like his argue that Southern countries should be compensated for their contribution to biotech.

Still others take a third position: that neither corporations nor indigenous peoples should claim ownership, because the gene pool ought not to be for sale, at any price. It should remain an open commons and continue to be used freely by present and future generations. They cite precedent in the recent historic decision by the nations of the world to maintain the continent of Antarctica as a global commons free from commercial exploitation.

Worldwide Protest

The idea of private companies laying claim to human genes as their exclusive intellectual property has resulted in growing protests worldwide. In May of 1994, a coalition of hundreds of women's organizations from more than forty nations announced opposition to Myriad Genetics' attempt to patent the gene that causes breast cancer in some women. The coalition was assembled by The Foundation on Economic Trends. While the women did not oppose the screening test Myriad developed, they opposed the claim to the gene itself. They argued that the breast cancer gene was a product of nature and not a human invention, and should not be patentable. Myriad's exclusive rights to such a gene could make screening more expensive, and might impede research by making access to the gene too expensive.

The central question in these cases—Can you patent life?—

is one of the most important issues ever to face the human family. Life patenting strikes at the core of our beliefs about the very nature of life and whether it is to be conceived as having sacred and intrinsic value, or merely utility value. Surely such a fundamental question deserves to be widely discussed by the public before such patents become a ubiquitous part of our daily lives.

The biotech revolution will force each of us to put a mirror to our most deeply held values, making us ponder the ultimate question of the purpose and meaning of existence. This may turn out to be its most important contribution. The rest is up to us.

| *"The [biotechnology] industry has no interest
in being declared the Creator of life."*

Some Patents on Genes Are Acceptable

Mark Sagoff

In the following viewpoint, Mark Sagoff maintains that scientists should be allowed to patent the genes they discover as well as the genetically modified cells and organisms produced in their laboratories. However, he emphasizes his belief that having a patent on a gene or organism should not imply that the scientist "owns," "invented," or "created" anything. Instead, patents are designed to encourage research by permitting patent owners to be the only ones legally permitted to profit from their discovery, for a limited period of time. Sagoff points out that plant breeders are allowed to patent the new varieties of plants that they develop, yet no one credits these plant breeders with "creating life." He suggests that laws regarding gene patents be amended to follow the language used in earlier laws regarding the patenting of hybrid plants. Mark Sagoff is a senior research fellow at the Institute for Philosophy and Public Policy at the University of Maryland.

As you read, consider the following questions:
1. What are the two purposes of patent law, according to Sagoff?
2. According to the author, in what way is the procedure for patenting hybrid plants different from the norm, as described in the Plant Patent Act of 1930 and the Plant Variety Protection Act of 1970?

Reprinted from Mark Sagoff, "Patented Genes: An Ethical Appraisal," *Issues in Science and Technology*, Spring 1998. Copyright ©1998 The University of Texas at Dallas, Richardson, TX. Reprinted with permission from *Issues in Science and Technology*.

On May 18, 1995, about 200 religious leaders representing 80 faiths gathered in Washington, D.C., to call for a moratorium on the patenting of genes and genetically engineered creatures. In their "Joint Appeal Against Human and Animal Patenting," the group stated: "We, the undersigned religious leaders, oppose the patenting of human and animal life forms. We are disturbed by the U.S. Patent Office's recent decision to patent body parts and several genetically engineered animals. We believe that humans and animals are creations of God, not humans, and as such should not be patented as human inventions."

Religious leaders, such as Ted Peters of the Center for Theology and Natural Sciences, argue that "patent policy should maintain the distinction between discovery and invention, between what already exists in nature and what human ingenuity creates. The intricacies of nature . . . ought not to be patentable." Remarks such as this worry the biotech industry, which has come to expect as a result of decisions over two decades by the U.S. Patent and Trademark Office (PTO) and by the courts that genes, cells, and multicellular animals are eligible for patent protection. The industry is concerned because religious leaders have considerable influence and because their point of view is consistent with the longtime legal precedent that products of nature are not patentable.

Representatives of the biotech industry argue that their religious critics fail to understand the purpose of patent law. According to the industry view, patents create temporary legal monopolies to encourage useful advances in knowledge; they have no moral or theological implications. As Biotechnology Industry Organization president Carl Feldbaum noted: "A patent on a gene does not confer ownership of that gene to the patent holder. It only provides temporary legal protections against attempts by other parties to commercialize the patent holder's discovery or invention." Lisa Raines, vice president of the Genzyme Corporation, summed up the industry view: "The religious leaders don't understand perhaps what our goals are. Our goals are not to play God; they are to play doctor."

The differences between the two groups are not irreconcilable. The religious leaders are not opposed to biotechnology, and the industry has no interest in being declared the Creator of life. The path to common ground must begin with an understanding of the two purposes of patent law.

The Two Purposes of Patent Law

Patent law traditionally has served two distinct purposes. First, it secures to inventors what one might call a natural property right to their inventions. "Justice gives every man a title to the product of his honest industry," wrote John Locke in his *Two Treatises on Civil Government.* If invention is an example of industry, then patent law recognizes a pre-existing moral right of inventors to own the products they devise, just as copyright recognizes a similar moral right of authors. Religious leaders, who believe that God is the author of nature (even if evolution may have entered the divine plan), take umbrage, therefore, when mortals claim to own what was produced by divine intelligence.

Second, patents serve the utilitarian purpose of encouraging technological progress by offering incentives—temporary commercial monopolies—for useful innovations. One could argue, as the biotech industry does, that these temporary monopolies are not intended to recognize individual genius but to encourage investments that are beneficial to society as a whole. Gene patents, if construed solely as temporary commercial monopolies, may make no moral claims about the provenance or authorship of life.

Legal practice in the past has avoided a direct conflict between these two purposes of patent policy—one moral, the other instrumental—in part by regarding products of nature as unpatentable because they are not "novel." For example, an appeals court in 1928 held that the General Electric Company could not patent pure tungsten but only its method for purifying it, because tungsten is not an invention but a "product of nature." In 1948, the Supreme Court in *Funk Brothers Seed Company v. Kalo Inoculant* invalidated a patent on a mixture of bacteria that did not occur together in nature. The Court stated that the mere combination of bacterial strains found separately in nature did not constitute "an invention or discovery within the meaning of the patent statutes." The Court wrote, "Patents cannot issue for the discovery of the phenomena of nature. . . . [They] are part of the storehouse of knowledge of all men. They are manifestations of laws of nature, free to all men and reserved exclusively to none."

The Case of Plant Breeding

The moral and instrumental purposes of patent law came into conflict earlier in this century when plant breeders, such as Luther Burbank, sought to control the commercial rights to the new varieties they produced. If patents served solely an instrumental purpose to encourage by rewarding useful labor and investment, one might say that patents should issue on the products of the breeder's art. Yet both the PTO and the courts denied patentability to the mere repackaging of genetic material found in nature because, as the Supreme Court said later about a hybridized bacterium, even if it "may have been the product of skill, it certainly was not the product of invention."

To put this distinction in Aristotelian terms, breeders provided the efficient cause (that is, the tools or labor needed to bring hybrids into being) but not the formal cause (that is, the design or structure of these varieties). Plant breeders could deposit samples of a hybrid with the patent office, but they could not describe the design or plan by which others could construct a plant variety from simpler materials. The patent statute requires, however, applicants to describe the design "in such full, clear, concise and exact terms as to enable any person skilled in the art to which it pertains . . . to make and use the same." A breeder could do little more to specify the structure of a new variety than to refer to its ancestor plants and to the methods used to produce it. This would represent no advance in plant science; it would tell others only what they already understood.

Confronted with the inapplicability of intellectual property law to new varieties of plants, Congress enacted the Plant Patent Act of 1930 and the Plant Variety Protection Act of 1970, which protect new varieties against unauthorized asexual and sexual reproduction, respectively. Breeders were required to deposit samples in lieu of providing a description of how to make the plant. Congress thus created commercial monopolies that implied nothing about invention and therefore nothing about moral or intellectual property rights. Accordingly, religious leaders had no reason to object to these laws.

The Court Changes Everything

This legal understanding concerning products of nature lasted until 1980, when the Supreme Court, by a 5–4 majority, decided in *Diamond v. Chakrabarty*, that Chakrabarty, a biologist, could patent hybridized bacteria because "his discovery is not nature's handiwork, but his own." The court did not intend to reverse the long tradition of decisions that held products of nature not to be patentable. The majority opinion reiterated that "a new mineral discovered in the earth or a new plant discovered in the wild is not patentable subject matter." The majority apparently believed that the microorganisms Chakrabarty wished to patent were not naturally occurring but resulted from "human ingenuity and research." The plaintiffs' lawyers failed to disabuse the court of this mistaken impression because they focused on the potential hazards of engineered organisms, a matter (as the Court held) that is irrelevant to their patentability.

Although Chakrabarty's patent disclosure, in its first sentence, claims that the microorganisms were "developed by the application of genetic engineering techniques," Chakrabarty had simply cultured different strains of bacteria together in the belief that they would exchange genetic material in a laboratory "soup" just as they do in nature. Chakrabarty himself was amazed at the Court's decision, since he had used commonplace methods that also occur naturally to exchange genetic material between bacteria. "I simply shuffled genes, changing bacteria that already existed," Chakrabarty told *People* magazine. "It's like teaching your pet cat a few new tricks."

A Major Change in Patent Policy

The Chakrabarty decision emboldened the biotechnology industry to argue that patents should issue on genes, proteins, and other materials that had commercial value. In congressional hearings on the Biotechnology Competitiveness Act, which passed in the Senate in 1988, witnesses testified that the United States was locked in a "global race against time to assure our eminence in biotechnology"; a race in which the PTO had an important role to play.

What Can and Cannot Be Patented

The U.S. Patent and Trademark Office does not patent things that exist naturally, such as the human genome. It grants intellectual property rights on human ingenuity that meets three criteria: novelty, nonobviousness, and utility. What is invented is patentable. What already exists in nature is not. Nor, despite widespread propaganda to the contrary, does the PTO patent human beings or body parts. No persons get patented. This would violate the U.S. Constitution's proscription against slavery. Rather, the PTO grants patents for cell lines and even genomes of transgenic animals that are used in biological research for the purpose of developing medical therapies for genetically based diseases such as cancer, heart disease, cystic fibrosis, Alzheimer's, Huntington's, Wilson's Syndrome, and eventually perhaps four thousand other diseases. Such patents draw venture capital for this extremely risky and expensive process of research and development. This is an area of ethical concern, to be sure, and one that deserves careful and informed deliberation by our religious leaders. It does not deserve categorical dismissal.

Ted Peters, *First Things*, May 1996.

While Congress was debating the issue, the PTO was already implementing a major change in policy. It began routinely issuing patents on products of nature (or functional equivalents), including genes, gene fragments and sequences, cell lines, human proteins, and other naturally occurring compounds. For example, in 1987, Genetics Institute, Inc., received a patent on human erythropoietin (EPO), a protein consisting of 165 amino acids that stimulate the production of red blood cells. Genetics Institute did not claim in any sense to have invented EPO; it had extracted a tiny amount of the naturally occurring polymer from thousands of gallons of urine. Similarly, Scripps Clinic patented a clotting agent, human factor VIII:C, a sample of which it had extracted from human blood.

Harvard University acquired a patent on glycoprotein 120 antigen (GP120), a naturally occurring protein on the coat of the human immunodeficiency virus. A human T cell antigen receptor has also been patented. Firms have received patents for hundreds of genes and gene fragments; they have applied for patents for thousands more. With few exceptions, the products of nature for which patents issued were not changed, redesigned, or improved to make them more useful. Indeed, the utility of these proteins, genes, and cells typically depends on their functional equivalence with naturally occurring substances. Organisms produced by conventional breeding techniques also now routinely receive conventional patents, even though they may exhibit no more inventive conception or design than those Burbank bred. The distinction between products of skill and of invention, which was once sufficient to keep breeders from obtaining ordinary patents, no longer matters in PTO policy. Invention is no longer required; utility is everything.

The Search for Common Ground

Opponents of patents on genetic materials generally support the progress of biotechnology. At a press conference, religious leaders critical of patenting "the intricacies of nature" emphasized that they did not object to genetic engineering; indeed, they applauded the work of the biotech industry. Bishop Kenneth Carder of the United Methodist Church said, "What we are objecting to is the ownership of the gene, not the process by which it is used." In a speech delivered to the Pontifical Academy of Sciences in 1994, Pope John Paul II hailed progress in genetic science and technology. Nevertheless, the Pope said: "We rejoice that numerous researchers have refused to allow discoveries made about the genome to be patented. Since the human body is not an object that can be disposed of at will, the results of research should be made available to the whole scientific community and cannot be the property of a small group."

Industry representatives and others who support gene patenting may respond to their religious critics in either of two ways. First, they may reply that replicated complementary DNA (cDNA) sequences, transgenic plants and animals, purified proteins, and other products of biotechnology would not exist without human intervention in nature. Hence they are novel inventions, not identical to God's creations. Second, industry representatives may claim that the distinction between "invention" and "discovery" is no longer relevant to patent policy, if it ever was. They may concede, then, that genetic materials are products of nature but argue that these discoveries are patentable compositions of matter nonetheless.

Consider the assertion that genes, gene sequences, and living things, if they are at all altered by human agency, are novel organisms and therefore not products of nature. This defense of gene patenting would encounter several difficulties. First, patents have issued on completely unaltered biological materials such as GP120. Second, the differences between the patented and the natural substance, where there are any, are unlikely to affect its utility. Rather, the value or usefulness of the biological product often depends on its functional identity to or equivalence with the natural product and not on any difference that can be ascribed to human design, ingenuity, or invention. Third, the techniques such as cDNA replication and the immortalization of cell lines by which biological material is gathered and reproduced have become routine and obvious. The result of employing these techniques, therefore, might be the product of skill, but not of invention.

Proponents of gene patenting might concede that genes, proteins, and other patented materials are indeed products of nature. They may argue with Carl Feldbaum that this concession is irrelevant, however, because patents "confer commercial rights, not ownership." From this perspective, which patent lawyers generally endorse, patenting makes no moral claim to invention, design, or authorship but only creates a legal monopoly to serve commercial purposes. Ownership remains with God. Accordingly, gene patents carry no greater moral implications than do the temporary monopolies plant breeders enjoy in the results of their investment and research.

Patents Have Traditionally Implied Intellectual Ownership

Although this reply may be entirely consistent with current PTO policy, legal and cultural assumptions for centuries have associated patents with invention and therefore with the ownership of intellectual property. These assumptions cannot be dismissed. First, patents confer the three defining incidents of ownership: the right to sell, the right to use, and the right to exclude. If someone produced and used, say, human EPO, it would be a violation of the Genetic Institute patent. But all human beings produce EPO as well as other patented proteins in our bodies. Does this mean we are infringing a patent? Of course not. But why not, when producing and using the same protein outside our bodies does infringe the patent? If a biotech firm patents a naturally occurring chemical compound for pesticidal use, does that mean that indigenous people who have used that chemical for centuries will no longer be allowed to extract and use it? That such questions arise suggests that patents confer real ownership of products of nature, not just abstract commercial rights.

Second, intuitive ties founded in legal and cultural history connect patents with the moral claim to intellectual property. For centuries the PTO followed the Supreme Court in insisting that "a product must be more than new and useful to be patented; it must also satisfy the requirements of invention." The requirements of invention included a contribution to useful knowledge—some display of ingenuity for which the inventor might take credit. By disclosing this new knowledge (rather than keeping it a trade secret), the inventor would contribute to and thus repay the store of knowledge on which he drew. One simply cannot scoff, as industry representatives sometimes do, at a centuries-long tradition of legal and cultural history, enshrined in every relevant Supreme Court decision, that connects intellectual property with moral claims based on contributions to knowledge.

Religious leaders who decry current PTO policy in granting intellectual property rights to products of nature have suggested alternative ways to give the biotech industry the kinds of commercial protections it seeks. Rabbi David Saperstein, director of the Religious Action Center of Reform Judaism in Washington, D.C., has proposed that ways be found "through contract laws and licensing procedures to protect the economic investment that people make. . . ." On the industry side, spokespersons have been eager to assure their clerical critics that they do not want to portray themselves as the authors of life. What industry wants, they argue, is not to upstage the Creator but to enjoy a legal regime that protects and encourages investment. Industry is concerned with utility and practical results; religious and other critics are understandably upset by the moral implications of current PTO policy.

The Outlines of a Compromise

It is not hard to see the outlines of a compromise. If Congress enacts a Genetic Patenting Act that removes the "description requirement" for genetic materials, as it has removed this requirement for hybridized plants, patents conferred on these materials may carry no implications about intellectual authorship. Such a statute, explicitly denying that biotech firms have invented or designed products of nature, might base gene patenting wholly on instrumental grounds and thus meet the objections of religious leaders.

A new statutory framework could accommodate all these concerns if it provided the kinds of monopoly commercial rights industry seeks without creating the implication or connotation that industry "invents," "designs," or "owns" genes as intellectual property. In other words, some middle ground modeled on the earlier plant protection acts might achieve a broad agreement among the parties now locked in dispute.

| *"Both cloning and embryo splitting have*
| *'no foreseeable ethically acceptable*
| *application to the human situation'*
| *and therefore should not be done."*

Human Cloning Should Be Banned

George Annas

George Annas is chair of the Department of Health Law at Boston University. On March 12, 1997, just a few weeks after it was reported that scientists had successfully cloned a sheep, Annas testified before Congress that cloning technology should not be applied to humans. In the following viewpoint, excerpted from his testimony, Annas maintains that human cloning is morally objectionable and that there is no good reason that experiments in human cloning should be allowed. Annas suggests that a federal agency be created to regulate all experiments involving humans. Such an agency, he believes, might permit experiments that involve cloning human cells for research purposes, but should not allow the resulting cloned embryos to be implanted into a human.

As you read, consider the following questions:
1. In Annas's words, why is the prospect of human cloning, "so simultaneously fascinating and horrifying"?
2. In Annas's opinion, why would human cloning *not* be protected by a constitutional right to reproduce?
3. What federal agency does the author suggest should be created to enforce regulations on research into human cloning?

Excerpted from George Annas, testimony before the Senate Committee on Labor and Human Resources Subcommittee on Public Health and Safety, March 12, 1997.

S enator Frist, thank you for the opportunity to appear before your subcommittee to address some of the legal and
ethical aspects surrounding the prospect of human cloning.
I agree with President [Bill] Clinton that we must "resist the
temptation to replicate ourselves" and that the use of federal
funds for the cloning of human beings should be prohibited.
On the other hand, the contours of any broader ban on human cloning require, I believe, sufficient clarity to permit at
least some research on the cellular level. This hearing provides an important opportunity to help explore and define
just what makes the prospect of human cloning so disturb-
ing to most Americans, and what steps the federal government can take to prevent the duplication of human beings
without preventing vital research from proceeding.

I will make three basic points this morning: (1) the negative reaction to the prospect of human cloning by the scientific, industrial and public sectors is correct because the
cloning of a human would cross a boundary that represents
a difference in kind rather than in degree in human "reproduction"; (2) there are no good or sufficient reasons to clone
a human; and (3) the prospect of cloning a human being provides an opportunity to establish a new regulatory framework for novel and extreme human experiments.

Altering the Very Definition of a Human Being

*1. The cloning of a human would cross a natural boundary that
represents a difference in kind rather than degree of human
"reproduction."*

There are those who worry about threats to biodiversity
by cloning animals, and even potential harm to the animals
themselves. But virtually all of the reaction to the appear-
ance of Dolly on the world stage has focused on the potential use of the new cloning technology to replicate a human
being. What is so simultaneously fascinating and horrifying
about this technology that produced this response? The answer is simple, if not always well-articulated: *replication of a
human by cloning would radically alter the very definition of a human being by producing the world's first human with a single genetic parent.* Cloning a human is also viewed as uniquely dis-
turbing because it is the manufacture of a person made to

order, represents the potential loss of individuality, and symbolizes the scientist's unrestrained quest for mastery over nature for the sake of knowledge, power, and profits.

Human cloning has been on the public agenda before, and we should recognize the concerns that have been raised by both scientists and policy makers over the past twenty-five years. In 1972, for example, the House Subcommittee on Science, Research and Development of the Committee on Science and Astronautics asked the Science Policy Research Division of the Library of Congress to do a study on the status of genetic engineering. Among other things, that report dealt specifically with cloning and parthenogenesis as it could be applied to humans. Although the report concluded that the cloning of human beings by nuclear substitution "is not now possible," it concluded that cloning "might be considered an advanced type of genetic engineering" if combined with the introduction of highly desirable DNA to "achieve some ultimate objective of genetic engineering." The Report called for assessment and detailed knowledge, forethought and evaluation of the course of genetic developments, rather than "acceptance of the haphazard evolution of the techniques of genetic engineering [in the hope that] the issues will resolve themselves."

Six years later, in 1978, the Subcommittee on Health and the Environment of the House Committee on Interstate and Foreign Commerce held hearings on human cloning in response to the publication of David Rorvick's *The Cloning of a Man*. All of the scientists who testified assured the committee that the supposed account of the cloning of a human being was fictional, and that the techniques described in the book could not work. One scientist testified that he hoped that by showing that the report was false it would also become apparent that the issue of human cloning itself "is a false one, that the apprehensions people have about cloning of human beings are totally unfounded." The major point the scientists wanted to make, however, was that they didn't want any regulations that might affect their research. In the words of one, "There is no need for any form of regulatory legislation, and it could only in the long run have a harmful effect."

Test-Tube Babies and Human Cloning

Congressional discussion of human cloning was interrupted by the birth of Baby Louise Brown, the world's first in vitro fertilization (IVF) baby, in 1978. The ability to conceive a child in a laboratory not only added a new way (in addition to artificial insemination) for humans to reproduce without sex, but also made it possible for the first time for a woman to gestate and give birth to a child to whom she had no genetic relationship. Since 1978, a child can have at least five parents: a genetic and rearing father, and a genetic, gestational, and rearing mother. We pride ourselves as having adapted to this brave new biological world, but in fact we have yet to develop reasonable and enforceable rules for even so elementary a question as who among these five possible parents the law should recognize as those with rights and obligations to the child. Many other problems, including embryo storage and disposition, posthumous use of gametes, and information available to the child also remain unresolved.

IVF represents a striking technological approach to infertility; nonetheless the child is still conceived by the union of an egg and sperm from two separate human beings of the opposite sex. Even though no change in the genetics and biology of embryo creation and growth is at stake in IVF, society continues to wrestle with fundamental issues involving this method of reproduction twenty years after its introduction. Viewing IVF as a precedent for human cloning misses the point. Over the past two decades many ethicists have been accused of "crying wolf" when new medical and scientific technologies have been introduced. This may have been the case in some instances, but not here. This change in kind in the fundamental way in which humans can "reproduce" represents such a challenge to human dignity and the potential devaluation of human life (even comparing the "original" to the "copy" in terms of which is to be more valued) that even the search for an analogy has come up empty-handed.

Cloning is replication, not reproduction, and represents a difference in kind not in degree in the manner in which human beings reproduce. Thus, although the constitutional right not to reproduce would seem to apply with equal force, to a right not to replicate, to the extent that there is a con-

stitutional right to reproduce (if one is able to), it seems unlikely that existing privacy or liberty doctrine would extend
this right to replication by cloning.

Echoes of *Frankenstein*

2. There are no good or sufficient reasons to clone a human.

When the President's Bioethics Commission reported on
genetic engineering in 1982 in their report entitled *Splicing
Life*, human cloning rated only a short paragraph in a footnote. The paragraph concluded: "The technology to clone a
human does not—and may never—exist. Moreover, the critical nongenetic influences on development make it difficult
to imagine producing a human clone who would act or appear 'identical'." The NIH Human Embryo Research panel
that reported on human embryo research in September 1994
also devoted only a single footnote to this type of cloning.
"Popular notions of cloning derive from science fiction
books and films that have more to do with cultural fantasies
than actual scientific experiments." Both of these expert
panels were wrong to disregard lessons from our literary
heritage on this topic, thereby attempting to sever science
from its cultural context.

Literary treatments of cloning help inform us that applying this technology to humans is too dangerous to human
life and values. The reporter who described Dr. Ian Wilmut
as "Dolly's laboratory father" couldn't have conjured up images of Mary Shelley's *Frankenstein* better if he had tried.
Frankenstein was also his creature's father/god; the creature
telling him: "I ought to be thy Adam." Like Dolly, the "spark
of life" was infused into the creature by an electric current.
Unlike Dolly, the creature was created as a fully grown adult
(not a cloning possibility, but what many Americans fanta-
size and fear), and wanted more than creaturehood: he
wanted a mate of his "own kind" with whom to live, and reproduce. Frankenstein reluctantly agreed to manufacture
such a mate if the creature agrees to leave humankind alone,
but in the end, viciously destroyed the female creature-mate,
concluding that he has no right to inflict the children of this
pair, "a race of devils," upon "everlasting generations."
Frankenstein ultimately recognized his responsibilities to

humanity, and Shelley's great novel explores virtually all the noncommercial elements of today's cloning debate.

The naming of the world's first cloned mammal also has great significance. The sole survivor of 277 cloned embryos (or "fused couplets"), the clone could have been named after its sequence number in this group (e.g., C-137), but this would have only emphasized its character as a produced product. In stark contrast, the name Dolly (provided for the public and not used in the scientific report in *Nature*) suggests an individual, a human or at least a pet. Even at the manufactured level a "doll" is something that produces great joy in our children and is itself harmless. Victor Frankenstein, of course, never named his creature, thereby repudiating any parental responsibility. The creature himself evolved into a monster when it was rejected not only by Frankenstein, but by society as well. Naming the world's first mammal-clone Dolly is meant to distance her from the Frankenstein myth both by making her appear as something she is not, and by assuming parental obligations toward her.

Why Bother to Clone Humans?

Unlike Shelley's, Aldous Huxley's *Brave New World* future in which all humans are created by cloning through embryo splitting and conditioned to join one of five worker groups, was always unlikely. There are much more efficient ways of creating killers or terrorists (or even workers) than through cloning—physical and psychological conditioning can turn teenagers into terrorists in a matter of months, rather than waiting some eighteen to twenty years for the clones to grow up and be trained themselves. Cloning has no real military or paramilitary uses. Even Hitler's clone would himself likely be quite a different person because he would grow up in a radically altered world environment.

It has been suggested, however, that there might be good reasons to clone a human. Perhaps most compelling is cloning a dying child if this is what the grieving parents want. But this should not be permitted. Not only does this encourage the parents to produce one child in the image of another, it also encourages all of us to view children as interchangeable commodities, because cloning is so different from human reproduction. When a child is cloned, it is not the parents that are being replicated (or are "reproducing") but the child. No one should have such dominion over a child (even a dead or dying child) as to be permitted to use its genes to create the child's child. Humans have a basic right not to reproduce, and human reproduction (even replication) is not like reproducing farm animals, or even pets. Ethical human reproduction properly requires the voluntary participation of the genetic parents. Such voluntary participation is not possible for a young child. Related human rights and dignity would also prohibit using cloned children as organ sources for their father/mother original. Nor is there any "right to be cloned" that an adult might possess that is triggered by marriage to someone with whom the adult cannot reproduce.

Reprinted with permission from Kirk Anderson.

Any attempt to clone a human being should also be prohibited by basic ethical principles that prohibit putting human subjects at significant risk without their informed consent. Dolly's birth was a one-in-277 embryo chance. The birth of a human from cloning might be technologically possible, but we could only discover this by unethically subjecting the planned child to the risk of serious genetic or physical injury, and subjecting a planned child to this type of risk could literally never be justified. Because we will likely never be able to protect the human subject of cloning research from serious harm, the basic ethical rules of human experimentation prohibit us from ever using it on humans.

Government Regulation Is Necessary

3. Developing a regulatory framework for human cloning

What should we do to prevent Dolly technology from being used to manufacture duplicate humans? We have three basic models for scientific/medical policy-making in the U.S.: the market, professional standards, and legislation. We tend to worship the first, distrust the second, and disdain the third. Nonetheless, the prospect of human cloning requires more deliberation about social and moral issues than either the market or science can provide. The market has no morality, and if we believe important values including issues of human rights and human dignity are at stake, we cannot leave cloning decisions to the market. The Biotechnology Technology Industry Organization in the U.S. has already taken the commendable position that human cloning should be prohibited by law. Science often pretends to be value-free, but in fact follows its own imperatives, and either out of ignorance or self-interest assumes that others are making the policy decisions about whether or how to apply the fruits of their labors. We disdain government involvement in reproductive medicine. But cloning is different in kind, and only government has the authority to restrain science and technology until its social and moral implications are adequately examined.

We have a number of options. The first is for Congress to simply ban the use of human cloning. Cloning for replication can (and should) be confined to nonhuman life. We need not, however, prohibit all possible research at the cellular level. For example, to the extent that scientists can make a compelling case for use of cloning technology on the cellular level for research on processes such as cell differentiation and senescence, and so long as any and all attempts to implant a resulting embryo into a human or other animal, or to continue cell division beyond a 14-day period are prohibited, use of human cells for research could be permitted. Anyone proposing such research, however, should have the burden of proving that the research is vital, cannot be conducted any other way, and is unlikely to produce harm to society.

The prospect of human cloning also provides Congress with the opportunity to go beyond ad hoc bans on procedures and funding, and the periodic appointment of blue ribbon committees, and to establish a Human Experimentation Agency with both rule-making and adjudicatory authority in the area of human experimentation. Such an agency could both promulgate rules governing human research and review and approve or disapprove research proposals in areas such as human cloning which local IRBs [institutional review boards] are simply incapable of providing meaningful reviews. The President's Bioethics panel is important and useful as a forum for discussion and possible policy development. But we have had such panels before, and it is time to move beyond discussion to meaningful regulation in areas like cloning where there is already a societal consensus.

Human Cloning Should Not Be Done

One of the most important procedural steps a federal Human Experimentation Agency should take is to put the burden of proof on those who propose to do extreme and novel experiments, such as cloning, that cross reorganized boundaries and call deeply held societal values into question. Thus, cloning proponents should have to prove that there is a compelling reason to approve research on it. I think the Canadian Royal Commission on New Reproductive Technologies quite properly concluded that both cloning and embryo splitting have "no foreseeable ethically acceptable application to the human situation" and therefore should not be done. We need an effective mechanism to ensure that it is not.

| "*Several fundamental constitutional principles conflict with any cloning ban.*"

Human Cloning Should Not Be Banned

Mark D. Eibert

In the following viewpoint, attorney Mark D. Eibert maintains that proposed bans on human cloning are unconstitutional. Since cloning would probably be used by infertile people as a means of reproduction, he writes, a ban on cloning would violate the legally recognized right to reproduce. In addition, Eibert contends that government interference in scientific inquiry is a violation of the rights to free speech and personal liberty. Moreover, Eibert predicts that in order to enforce a ban on human cloning, the government would have to be given enormous power to monitor the actions of research laboratories and infertility clinics. Since, in his view, human cloning would be a harmless procedure, Eibert concludes that talk of banning the technology should be abandoned.

As you read, consider the following questions:
1. In the author's opinion, for infertile people, a ban on cloning would be the equivalent of what?
2. According to the author, why has the government traditionally not outlawed potentially dangerous reproductive technologies?
3. What problems would there be in enforcing a ban on human cloning, in Eibert's view?

"There are some avenues that should be off limits to science. If scientists will not draw the line for themselves, it is up to the elected representatives of the people to draw it for them."

Thus declared Senator Christopher "Kit" Bond (R-Mo.) one of the sponsors of S. 1601, the official Republican bill to outlaw human cloning. The bill would impose a 10-year prison sentence on anyone who uses "human somatic cell nuclear transfer technology" to produce an embryo, even if only to study cloning in the laboratory. If enacted into law, the bill would effectively ban all research into the potential benefits of human cloning. Scientists who use the technology for any reason—and infertile women who use it to have children—would go to jail.

The Race to Ban Human Cloning

Not to be outdone, Democrats have come up with a competing bill. Senators Ted Kennedy (Mass.) and Dianne Feinstein (Calif.) have proposed S. 1602, which would ban human cloning for at least 10 years. It would allow scientists to conduct limited experiments with cloning in the laboratory, provided any human embryos are destroyed at an early stage rather than implanted into a woman's uterus and allowed to be born.

If the experiment goes too far, the Kennedy-Feinstein bill would impose a $1 million fine and government confiscation of all property, real or personal, used in or derived from the experiment. The same penalties that apply to scientists appear to apply to new parents who might use the technology to have babies.

The near unanimity on Capitol Hill about the need to ban human cloning makes it likely that some sort of bill will be voted on this session and that it will seriously restrict scientists' ability to study human cloning. [As of February 2000, no federal laws have been enacted that restrict research into cloning.] In the meantime, federal bureaucrats have leapt into the breach. In January 1998, the U.S. Food and Drug Administration announced that it planned to "regulate" (that is, prohibit) human cloning. In the past, the FDA has largely ignored the fertility industry, making no effort to regulate in vitro fertilization, methods for injecting sperm into eggs, and other advanced reproductive technologies that have much in common with cloning techniques.

An FDA spokesperson told me that although Congress never expressly granted the agency jurisdiction over cloning, the FDA can regulate it under its statutory authority over biological products (like vaccines or blood used in transfusions) and drugs. But even Representative Vernon Ehlers (R-Mich.), one of the most outspoken congressional opponents of cloning, admits that "it's hard to argue that a cloning procedure is a drug." Of course, even if Congress had granted the FDA explicit authority to regulate cloning, such authority would only be valid if Congress had the constitutional power to regulate reproduction—which is itself a highly questionable assumption (more on that later).

Nor have state legislatures been standing still. Effective January 1, 1998, California became the first state to outlaw human cloning. California's law defines "cloning" so broadly and inaccurately—as creating children by the transfer of nuclei from *any* type of cell to enucleated eggs—that it also bans a promising new infertility treatment that has nothing to do with cloning. In that new procedure, doctors transfer nuclei from older, dysfunctional eggs (not differentiated adult cells as in cloning) to young, healthy donor eggs, and then inseminate the eggs with the husband's sperm—thus conceiving an ordinary child bearing the genes of both parents. Taking California as their bellwether, many other states are poised to follow in passing very restrictive measures.

Cloning Bans and the Constitution

What started this unprecedented governmental grab for power over both human reproduction and scientific inquiry? Within days after Dolly, the cloned sheep, made her debut, President Clinton publicly condemned human cloning. He opined that "any discovery that touches upon human creation is not simply a matter of scientific inquiry. It is a matter of morality and spirituality as well. Each human life is unique, born of a miracle that reaches beyond laboratory science."

Clinton then ordered his National Bioethics Advisory Commission to spend all of 90 days studying the issue—after which the board announced that it agreed with Clinton. Thus, Clinton succeeded in framing the debate this way: Human cloning was inherently bad, and the federal government had the power to outlaw it.

Federal Law Has Traditionally Stayed Out of Bioethical Debates

The idea that federal criminal law is needed to prevent potential harmful or unethical uses of a reproductive or other medical innovation is unique in bioethics. Most federal bioethical regulation has occurred through the federal funding power, not through the use of direct criminal sanctions. For example, the extensive federal regulation of human subjects research has occurred in the guise of the conditional spending power. . . .

Indeed, many harmful and dangerous practices now occur in medicine without federal criminal sanctions. Physician assisted suicide and active euthanasia, which doubtlessly occur to some extent, directly harm patients but there is no federal criminal law against it. Many surgical procedures are performed on patients without adequate review of safety, yet there are no federal criminal sanctions against them. One exception is a law that makes abortion with intent to provide fetal tissue for transplant a crime. This provision was added as part of a legislative compromise to enable federal funding of fetal tissue transplantation research to occur, and is arguably unconstitutional.

Of course, the fact that federal criminal law has rarely been used in the bioethical area is no argument against using it now if there is a strong case for doing so. But it is precisely such a strong case that is lacking.

John Robertson, quoted in Gregory E. Pence, ed., *Flesh of My Flesh: The Ethics of Cloning Humans*. New York: Rowman & Littlefield, 1998.

But in fact, it's far from clear that the government has such far-reaching authority. Several fundamental constitutional principles conflict with any cloning ban. Chief among them are the right of adults to have children and the right of scientists to investigate nature.

The Right to Procreate

The Supreme Court has ruled that every American has a constitutional right to "bear or beget" children. This includes the right of infertile people to use sophisticated medical technologies like in vitro fertilization. As the U.S. District Court for the Northern District of Illinois explained, "Within the cluster of constitutionally protected choices that includes the right to have access to contraceptives, there must be included . . . the right to submit to a medical procedure that may bring about, rather than prevent, pregnancy."

About 15 percent of Americans are infertile, and doctors often cannot help them. Federal statistics show that in vitro fertilization and related technologies have an average national success rate of less than 20 percent. Similarly, a *Consumer Reports* study concludes that fertility clinics produce babies for only 25 percent of patients. That leaves millions of people who still cannot have children, often because they can't produce viable eggs or sperm, even with fertility drugs. Until recently, their only options have been to adopt or to use eggs or sperm donated by strangers.

Once cloning technology is perfected, however, infertile individuals will no longer need viable eggs or sperm to conceive their own genetic children—any body cell will do. Thus, cloning may soon offer many Americans the only way possible to exercise their constitutional right to reproduce. For them, cloning bans are the practical equivalent of forced sterilization.

In 1942, the Supreme Court struck down a law requiring the sterilization of convicted criminals, holding that procreation is "one of the basic civil rights of man," and that denying convicts the right to have children constitutes "irreparable injury" and "forever deprived [them] of a basic liberty." To uphold a cloning ban, then, a court would have to rule that naturally infertile citizens have less right to try to have children than convicted rapists and child molesters do.

Prohibiting Cloning Would Be a Form of Eugenics

Many politicians and bureaucrats who want to ban human cloning say they need their new powers to "protect" children. Reciting a long list of speculative harms, ranging from possible physical deformities to the psychic pain of being an identical twin, they argue in essence that cloned children would be better off never being born at all.

But politicians and the media have grossly overstated the physical dangers of cloning. The Dolly experiment started with 277 fused eggs, of which only 29 became embryos. All the embryos were transferred to 13 sheep. One became pregnant, with Dolly. The success rate per uterine transfer (one perfect offspring from 13 sheep, with no miscarriages) was better than the early success rates for in vitro fertilization. Subsequent animal experiments in Wisconsin have already made the process much more efficient, and improvements will presumably continue as long as further research is allowed. More fundamentally, the government does not have the constitutional authority to decide who gets born—although it once thought it did, a period that constitutes a dark chapter of our national heritage. In the early 20th century, 30 states adopted eugenics laws, which required citizens with conditions thought to be inheritable (insanity, criminal tendencies, retardation, epilepsy, etc.) to be sterilized—partly as a means of "protecting" the unfortunate children from being born.

In 1927, the U.S. Supreme Court upheld such a law, with Oliver Wendell Holmes writing for the majority, "It would be better for all the world, if instead of waiting to execute degenerate offspring for crime, or to let them starve for their imbecility, society can prevent those who are manifestly unfit from continuing their kind. . . . Three generations of imbeciles are enough."

California's eugenics law in particular was admired and emulated in other countries—including Germany in 1933. But during and after World War II, when Americans learned how the Nazis had used their power to decide who was "perfect" enough to be born, public and judicial opinion about eugenics began to shift. By the 1960s, most of the eugenics laws in this country had been either repealed, fallen into disuse, or were struck down as violating constitutional guarantees of due process and equal protection.

Parents, Not Government, Should Decide

Indeed, those old eugenics laws were a brief deviation from an American tradition that has otherwise been unbroken for over 200 years. In America, it has always been the prospective parents, never the government, who decided how much risk was acceptable for a mother and her baby—even where the potential harm was much more certain and serious than anything threatened by cloning.

Hence, in vitro fertilization and fertility drugs are legal, even though they create much higher risks of miscarriages, multiple births, and associated birth defects. Individuals who themselves have or are known carriers of serious inheritable mental or physical defects such as sickle cell anemia, hemophilia, cystic fibrosis, muscular dystrophy, and Tay-Sachs disease are allowed to reproduce, naturally and through in vitro fertilization, even though they risk having babies with serious, or even fatal, defects or diseases. Older mothers at risk of having babies with Down Syndrome, and even women with AIDS, are also allowed to reproduce, both naturally and artificially. Even if prenatal testing shows a fetus to have a serious defect like Down Syndrome, no law requires the parents to abort it to save it from a life of suffering.

In short, until science revealed that human cloning was possible, society assumed that prospective parents could decide for themselves and their unborn children how much risk and suffering were an acceptable part of life. But in the brave new world of the federal bureaucrat, that assumption no longer holds true.

Ironically, some cloning opponents have turned the eugenics argument on its head, contending that cloning could lead to "designer children" and superior beings who might one day rule mankind. But allowing infertile individuals to conceive children whose genome is nearly identical to their already existing genomes no more creates "designer children" than it creates "designer parents." More important, these opponents miss the point that only government has the broad coercive power over society as a whole necessary to make eugenics laws aimed at "improving the race." It is those who support laws to ban cloning who are in effect urging the passage of a new eugenics law, not those who want to keep government out of the business of deciding who is perfect enough or socially desirable enough to be born.

Another significant driving force behind attempts to restrict or reverse an expansion in human knowledge stems from religious convictions. Interestingly, there is no necessary theological opposition to cloning: For example, two leading rabbis and a Muslim scholar who testified before the National Bioethics Advisory Commission had no objection to the practice and even advanced religious arguments *for* cloning.

Still, politicians from both major parties have already advanced religious arguments against cloning. President Clinton wants to outlaw cloning as a challenge to "our cherished concepts of faith and humanity." [1998] House Majority Leader Dick Armey also opposes cloning, saying that "to be human is to be made in the image and likeness of a loving God," and that "creating multiple copies of God's unique handiwork" is bad for a variety of reasons. Senator Bond warns that "humans are not God and they should not be allowed to play God"—a formulation similar to that of Albert Moraczewski, a theologian with the National Conference of Catholic Bishops, who told the president's commission, "Cloning exceeds the limits of the delegated dominions given to the human race."

Of course, virtually every major medical, scientific, and technological advance in modern history was initially criticized as "playing God." To give just two recent examples, heart transplants and "test tube babies" both faced religious opposition when first introduced. Today, heart transplants save 2,000 lives every year, and in vitro fertilization helped infertile Americans have 11,000 babies in 1995 alone.

Religious belief doesn't require opposition to these sorts of expansions in human knowledge and technology. And basing a cloning ban primarily on religious grounds would seem to violate the Establishment Clause. But that's not the only potential constitutional problem with a ban.

The Rights to Free Speech and Personal Liberty Protect Scientific Inquiry

Many courts and commentators say that a constitutional right of scientific inquiry is inherent in the rights of free speech and personal liberty. To be sure, certain governmental attempts to restrict the methods scientists can use have been upheld—for example, regulations requiring free and informed consent by experimental subjects. But those have to do with protecting the rights of others. Cloning bans try to stop research that everyone directly concerned wants to continue. As one member of the National Bioethics Advisory Commission observed, if the group's recommendation to ban cloning is enacted, it would apparently be the first time in American history that an entire field of medical research has been outlawed.

Prohibiting scientific and medical activities would also raise troubling enforcement issues. How exactly would the FBI—in its new role as "reproductive police" and scientific overseer—learn, then prove, that scientists, physicians, or parents were violating the ban? Would they raid research laboratories and universities? Seize and read the private medical records of infertility patients? Burst into operating rooms with their guns drawn? Grill new mothers about how their babies were conceived? Offer doctors reduced sentences for testifying against the patients whose babies they delivered? And would the government really confiscate, say, Stanford University Medical Center, if one of its many researchers or clinicians "goes too far"?

The year since the announcement of Dolly's birth has seen unprecedented efforts by government to expand its power over both human reproduction and science. Decisions traditionally made by individuals—such as whether and how to have children, or to study the secrets of nature—have suddenly been recast as political decisions to be made in Washington.

No Reason to Fear Human Cloning

Human cloning, when it actually arrives, is not apt to have dire consequences. Children conceived through cloning technology will be not "Xerox copies" but unique individuals with their own personalities and full human rights. Once this basic fact is understood, the only people likely to be interested in creating children through cloning technology are incurably infertile individuals. There are already tens of millions of identical twins walking the earth, and they have posed no threat so far to God, the family, or country. A few more twins, born to parents who desperately want to have, raise, and love them as their own children, will hardly be noticed.

As for the nightmare fantasies spun by cloning opponents, even the president's special commission has admitted that fears of cloning being used to create hordes of Hitlers or armies of identical slaves are "based . . . on gross misunderstandings of human biology and psychology." And laws already prohibit criminal masterminds from holding slaves, abusing children, or cutting up people for spare body parts.

As harmless as the fact of cloning may be, the fear of cloning is already bearing bitter fruit: unprecedented extensions of government power, based either on unlikely nightmare scenarios or on an unreasoning fear that humans were "not meant" to know or do certain things. Far from protecting the "sanctity" of human life, such an attitude, if consistently applied, would doom the human race to a "natural" state of misery.

Periodical Bibliography

The following articles have been selected to supplement the diverse views presented in this chapter. Addresses are provided for periodicals not indexed in the *Readers' Guide to Periodical Literature*, the *Alternative Press Index*, the *Social Sciences Index*, or the *Index to Legal Periodicals and Books*.

Ronald Bailey	"Petri Dish Politics," *Reason*, December 1999.
Ronald Bailey	"The Twin Paradox: What Exactly Is Wrong with Cloning People?" *Reason*, May 1997.
CQ Researcher	"The Cloning Controversy," May 9, 1997.
CQ Researcher	"Embryo Research," December 17, 1999.
Gregg Easterbrook	"Medical Evolution: Will Homo Sapiens Become Obsolete?" *New Republic*, March 1, 1999.
Stephen S. Hall	"The Recycled Generation," *New York Times Magazine*, January 30, 2000.
Hastings Center Report	"Religious Voices in Biotechnology: The Case of Gene Patenting," November/December 1997.
Robert Marantz Henig	"The Rush to Build a Better Human Being," *Washington Post*, January 17, 2000.
Leon Kass	"The Wisdom of Repugnance: Why We Should Ban the Cloning of Humans," *New Republic*, June 2, 1997.
Ruth Macklin	"Human Cloning? Don't Just Say No," *U.S. News & World Report*, March 10, 1997.
John J. Miller	"Hard Cell," *National Review*, April 5, 1999.
Richard Powers	"Too Many Breakthroughs," *New York Times*, November 19, 1998.

Glossary

allele One of several possible forms of a **gene**, found on the same location on a **chromosome**, which can give rise to noticeably different hereditary characteristics.

amniocentesis A surgical procedure in which a syringe is used to draw a sample of the amniotic fluid surrounding a growing human fetus; by examining the fetal cells suspended in this fluid, physicians can test for possible genetic abnormalities in the fetus.

biotechnology A broad term that can include **genetic engineering**, reproductive technology, and the use of genetic technology to address environmental problems and to develop agricultural products.

Bt Abbreviation for the bacterium *Bacillus thuringiensis*. **Transgenic** Bt crops have a **gene** from the bacterium that causes them to produce a common agricultural insecticide.

chromosome A chain of genetic material in the cell **nucleus**, consisting of **DNA**, **RNA**, and **protein**. Humans have 26 pairs of chromosomes.

clone A **gene**, cell, bacterium, or other organism that is genetically identical to the parent cell from which it was produced; also, to create such genetic replicas.

differentiated cells Cells that have been genetically programmed by the body to become a certain type of tissue. See also **stem cells**.

DNA (deoxyribonucleic acid) The molecule that is the basic genetic material found in all living things.

dominant A genetic trait that is apparent even if only one parent contributes the **allele** associated with it.

embryo The developing organism from the time of fertilization until significant differentiation has occurred, when it becomes known as the fetus.

eugenics The science of improving a breed or species, especially the human species, either through **genetic engineering** or by encouraging reproduction by persons presumed to have desirable genetic traits.

gene A specialized segment of **DNA** whose sequence encodes the structure of a **protein**; genes are responsible for all the inherited characteristics of an organism.

gene pool All the **genes** in a given population of organisms.

gene therapy A form of human **genetic engineering** in which **genes** are inserted into cells in an attempt to overcome the effects of defective genes that cause disease.

genetic engineering A technology used to alter the genetic material of living things.

genetic enhancement The use of **genetic engineering** to improve an organism or species. Genetic enhancement is often associated with **eugenics** and contrasted with **gene therapy**.

genetic screening The testing of individuals, fetuses, **embryos**, or sperm or egg cells for genetic abnormalities.

genetics The branch of biology dealing with **heredity** and variation in organisms.

gene transfer See **genetic engineering**.

genome The complete set of **genes** in an organism.

germ-line gene therapy The insertion of **genes** into a sperm cell, egg cell, or fertilized egg; genetic alterations made in germ-line gene therapy will affect all the cells in the future person's body and will be passed onto the person's offspring.

heredity The transmission of characteristics from parents to offspring.

Human Genome Project The federally funded initiative to map and sequence the entire human **genome**.

in vitro A biological process conducted in a nonliving environment, such as in a laboratory vessel; contrasted with in vivo processes that occur within living organisms.

in vitro fertilization (IVF) A reproductive technology by which an egg cell is fertilized with sperm in a laboratory dish and the resulting **embryo** is later implanted in a uterus for gestation; IVF embryos are often the proposed subjects for **germ-line gene therapy** and **genetic screening**.

nucleus The part of a cell that contains the **chromosomes** and the bulk of the cell's **DNA**.

polygenic A physical trait that is affected by more than one **gene**; most human traits are thought to be polygenic.

protein A broad term used to describe many of the organic molecules that constitute a large portion of the mass of every organism; each **gene** in an organism encodes one protein.

rBST (recombinant bovine somatotropin) A cow hormone, which bacteria have been genetically engineered to produce, that is used to increase milk production in dairy cows.

recessive A genetic trait that cannot become noticeable unless both parents contribute the **allele** that is associated with it.

recombinant DNA A segment of **DNA** in which one or more segments or **genes** have been inserted, either naturally or by laboratory manipulation. The new DNA may be from a different organism or from a different DNA segment of the same organism; in either case the result is a new genetic combination.

RNA (ribonucleic acid) Molecules made from and closely resembling **DNA**; these molecules carry messages from DNA to the rest of the cell, and they may be used in **gene therapy** to introduce foreign DNA into the **nucleus**.

somatic cell Any cell of an organism that is not destined to become a reproductive cell; in somatic-cell gene therapy, a person's cells are genetically altered but the altered **DNA** is not passed on to the person's children.

stem cells Cells that are capable of becoming any type of tissue in an organism, or of giving rise to a separate organism. See also **differentiated cells**.

transgenic Having genetic material that was introduced from another species.

For Further Discussion

Chapter 1

1. In describing the potential benefits of genetic engineering, David A. Christopher focuses heavily on the genetic engineering of plants, animals, bacteria, and vaccines. In contrast, Jeremy Rifkin emphasizes the dangers of genetically engineering humans. Based on their viewpoints, do you think Christopher would approve of genetically enhancing humans in the way Rifkin describes? Do you think Rifkin would take issue with the genetic engineering of bacteria and vaccines that Christopher describes? Explain your answer.

2. Eric S. Grace describes ways in which biotechnology could be used to treat disease. One of Jeffrey Klein's chief concerns about biotechnology is that corporations may misuse it in an effort to make a profit. Do you feel that Klein's concerns are valid? In your opinion, do his concerns outweigh the benefits Grace describes? How might the abuses Klein describes be prevented?

Chapter 2

1. Oliver Morton maintains that most people object to genetic engineering on the grounds that it is "unnatural." In your opinion, is this the basis for Bernard Gert's argument that the genetic engineering of humans is largely unethical? List the reasons that Gert opposes genetic enhancement of humans, and the reason that Morton favors it. In your opinion, who makes the more persuasive argument?

2. Ted Peters argues that as genetic researchers discover more disease-causing genes, prenatal genetic screening for these genes will result in an increase in the abortion rate. Walter Glannon suggests that genetic testing of embryos created through in vitro fertilization could help alleviate this problem—instead of aborting a fetus with a disease-causing gene, doctors instead could choose to implant the "test-tube" embryo that they know does not have such a gene. However, most people procreate through sex, rather than using in vitro fertilization. How does this fact affect your opinion of Glannon's argument?

3. Lee M. Silver argues that the real reasons people oppose human cloning are based on religious beliefs. After reading E.V. Kontorovich's viewpoint, do you agree with Silver's claim? Does Kontorovich make any convincing arguments that are not based on religion, and if so, what are they? Does Kontorovich

make any religious arguments against human cloning that you find persuasive?

Chapter 3

1. Ronnie Cummins lists a variety of ways in which genetically engineered food might harm human health or the environment. Which, if any, of these dangers do you find most worrisome? Thomas R. DeGregori argues that fears about genetically modified food are misguided. Do you find his arguments convincing? Explain your answer.

2. Why does Thomas R. DeGregori oppose the labeling of genetically altered food? Do you agree with his reasoning, or would you support regulations that would mandate special labels for foods produced from genetically altered crops and livestock?

3. Norman Borlaug believes that since biotechnology could help increase the food supply, it is irresponsible for activists in affluent nations to oppose genetic engineering in agriculture. Brian Halweil, on the other hand, believes that traditional methods of farming are superior to the use of genetically engineered crops. Based on their viewpoints, do you support the ban on genetically engineered crops and the transition to organic farming that Ronnie Cummins proposes at the end of her viewpoint? Why or why not?

Chapter 4

1. After the first cases of recombining DNA in the 1970s, scientists proceeded with caution—they called for a temporary moratorium on certain kinds of research and set ethical guidelines for others. Jane Maienschein concludes that this cautious approach is again warranted by advances in biotechnology, which in her view have a great potential for abuse. James D. Watson, the co-discoverer of the structure of DNA and the first director of the Human Genome Project, argues that this caution was unnecessary. He maintains that the enormous benefits of genetic engineering outweigh the potential hazards, and that regulation only slows progress. Whose argument do you find more convincing, and why?

2. Considering the viewpoints by Jeremy Rifkin and Mark Sagoff, do you feel that biotechnology companies should be allowed to patent genetically modified bacteria? What about genetically modified plants? Animals? Human genes? Explain your answer.

3. George Annas proposes that a federal Human Experimentation

Agency be created to enforce a partial ban on human cloning. Do you agree that such an organization is necessary? What objections would Mark D. Eibert have to this proposal?

4. Mark D. Eibert claims that a ban on human cloning would violate an infertile couple's right to reproduce through the use of medical technology. How would Annas respond to this claim? Do you feel that infertile couples should have access to human cloning? Explain.

Organizations to Contact

The editors have compiled the following list of organizations concerned with the issues debated in this book. The descriptions are derived from materials provided by the organizations. All have publications or information available for interested readers. The list was compiled on the date of publication of the present volume; the information provided here may change. Be aware that many organizations take several weeks or longer to respond to inquiries, so allow as much time as possible.

Alliance for BioIntegrity
406 W. Depot Ave., Fairfield, IA 52556
(515) 472-5554
e-mail: info@biointegrity.org • website: www.biointegrity.org

The Alliance for BioIntegrity is a nonprofit organization that opposes the use of genetic engineering in agriculture and works to educate the public about the dangers of genetically modified foods. Position papers that argue against genetic engineering from legal, religious, and scientific perspectives—including "Why the Genetic Engineering of Our Food Offends Principles of Most Religions" and information on the alliance's lawsuit against the Food and Drug Administration—are available on its website.

The BioDemocracy Campaign and Organic Consumers Association
6114 Highway 61, Little Marais, MN 55614
(218) 226-4164 • fax: (218) 226-4157
website: www.purefood.org

The BioDemocracy Campaign and Organic Consumers Association is an alliance between two advocacy groups that promotes food safety, organic farming, and sustainable agriculture practices. It provides information on the hazards of genetically engineered food, irradiated food, food grown with toxic sludge fertilizer, mad cow disease, rBGH in milk, and other issues, and organizes boycotts and protests around these issues. It publishes *BioDemocracy News* and its website includes many fact sheets and articles on genetically modified foods.

Biotechnology Industry Organization (BIO)
1625 K St. NW, Suite 1100, Washington, DC 20006
(202) 857-0244
website: www.bio.org

The Biotechnology Industry Organization represents biotechnology companies, academic institutions, state biotechnology centers, and related organizations that support the use of biotechnology in improving health care, agriculture, efforts to clean up the environment, and other fields. BIO works to educate the public about biotechnology and responds to concerns about the safety of genetic engineering and other technologies. It publishes the magazine *Your World, Our World,* and an introductory guide to biotechnology is available on its website.

Center for Bioethics and Human Dignity (CBHD)
2065 Half Day Rd., Bannockburn, IL 60015
(847) 317-8180 • fax: (847) 317-8153
website: www.bioethix.org

CBHD is an international education center whose purpose is to bring Christian perspectives to bear on contemporary bioethical challenges facing society. Its publications address genetic technologies as well as other topics such as euthanasia and abortion. It publishes the newsletter *Dignity* and the book *Genetic Ethics: Do the Ends Justify the Genes?*

Center for Bioethics at the University of Pennsylvania
3401 Market St., Suite 320, Philadelphia, PA 19104-3308
(215) 898-7136 • fax: (215) 573-3036
website: http://bioethics.net

The University of Pennsylvania's Center for Bioethics is the largest center of its kind in the world. It engages in research and publishes articles about many areas of bioethics, including gene therapy and genetic engineering. *PennBioethics* is its quarterly newsletter.

Council for Responsible Genetics (CRG)
5 Upland Rd., Suite 3, Cambridge, MA 02140
(617) 868-0870 • fax: (617) 491-5344
e-mail: marty@gene-watch.org • website: www.gene-watch.org

The Council for Responsible Genetics is a national nonprofit organization of scientists and public health advocates and others which promotes a comprehensive public interest agenda for biotechnology. Its members work to raise public awareness about genetic discrimination, patenting life forms, food safety, and environmental quality.

Foundation on Economic Trends (FET)
1660 L St. NW, Suite 216, Washington, DC 20036
(202) 466-2823 • fax: (202) 429-9602
website: www.biotechcentury.org

Founded by science critic and author Jeremy Rifkin, the foundation is a nonprofit organization whose mission is to examine emerging trends in science and technology and their impacts on the environment, the economy, culture, and society. FET works to educate the public about topics such as gene patenting, commercial eugenics, genetic discrimination, and genetically altered food. Its website contains articles and news updates, including information about FET's class-action lawsuit against Monsanto concerning that company's marketing of genetically modified seeds for agriculture.

The Hastings Center
Route 9D, Garrison, NY 10524-5555
(914) 424-4040 • fax: (914) 424-4545
website: www.hastingscenter.org

The Hastings Center is an independent research institute that explores the medical, ethical, and social ramifications of biomedical advances. The center publishes books, papers, and the bimonthly *Hastings Center Report*.

Human Cloning Foundation
PMB 143, 1100 Hammond Dr., Suite 410A, Atlanta, GA 30328
website: www.humancloning.org

The foundation is a nonprofit organization that promotes education about human cloning and other forms of biotechnology and emphasizes the positive aspects of these technologies. Its website contains numerous articles and fact sheets on the benefits of human cloning.

International Forum for Genetic Engineering (IfGene)
25126 Pleasant Hill Dr., Corvallis, OR 97333
(541) 929-3045
website: www.anth.org/ifgene

IfGene works to encourage a deeper dialogue about genetic engineering by giving special attention to the worldviews out of which people approach science and the moral and spiritual implications of biotechnology. The forum's website includes many articles on the ethics of genetic engineering, and IfGene's student help desk aids students on assignments, projects, or debates on genetic engineering or biotechnology.

National Bioethics Advisory Commission (NBAC)
6100 Executive Blvd., Suite 5B01, Rockville, MD 20592-7508
(301) 402-4242 • fax: (301) 480-6900
website: www.bioethics.gov

NBAC is a federal agency which sets guidelines that govern the ethical conduct of research. It works to protect the rights and welfare of human research subjects and governs the management and use of genetic information. Its published reports include *Cloning Human Beings* and *Ethical Issues in Human Stem Cell Research*.

National Institutes of Health
National Human Genome Research Institute (NHGRI)
9000 Rockville Pike, Bethesda, MD 20892
(301) 402-0911 • fax: (301) 402-0837
website: www.nhgri.nih.gov

NIH is the federal government's primary agency for the support of biomedical research. As a division of NIH, NHGRI's mission is to head the Human Genome Project, the federally funded effort to map all human genes. Information about the Human Genome Project is available at NHGRI's website.

U.S. Department of Agriculture (USDA)
14th & Independence Ave. SW, Washington, DC 20250
website on agricultural biotechnology: www.aphis.usda.gov/
biotechnology

The USDA is one of three federal agencies, along with the Environmental Protection Agency (EPA) and the U.S. Food and Drug Administration (FDA), primarily responsible for regulating biotechnology in the United States. The USDA conducts research on the safety of genetically engineered organisms, helps form government policy on agricultural biotechnology, and provides information to the public about these technologies.

Additional Internet Resources
These following are not run by specific organizations, but contain information that may be useful to students interested in learning more about genetic engineering.
Cold Spring Harbor's Primer on the Basics of DNA and Heredity
website: http://vector.cshl.org/dnaftb
Future Generations
website: www.eugenics.net
W. French Anderson's Gene Therapy
website: www.frenchanderson.org

Bibliography of Books

| Luke Anderson | *Genetic Engineering, Food, and Our Environment.* New York: Chelsea Green, 1999. |

Bryan Appleyard — *Brave New Worlds: Staying Human in the Genetic Future.* New York: Viking, 1998.

Ronald Cole-Turner, ed. — *Human Cloning: Religious Responses.* Louisville, KY: Westminster John Knox, 1997.

Timothy J. Demy and Gary P. Stewart, eds. — *Genetic Engineering: A Christian Response: Crucial Considerations in Shaping Life.* Grand Rapids, MI: Kregel, 1999.

Michael W. Fox — *Beyond Evolution: The Genetically Altered Future of Plants, Animals, the Earth, and Humans.* New York: Lyons, 1999.

Eric S. Grace — *Biotechnology Unzipped: Promises and Realities.* Washington, DC: Joseph Henry, 1997.

Mae-Wan Ho — *Genetic Engineering: Dream or Nightmare?* Bath, UK: Gateway, 1998.

Leon R. Kass and James Q. Wilson — *The Ethics of Human Cloning.* Washington, DC: AEI, 1998.

John F. Kilner, Rebecca D. Pentz, and Frank E. Young — *Genetic Ethics: Do the Ends Justify the Genes?* Grand Rapids, MI: William B. Eerdmans, 1997.

Andrew Kimbrell — *The Human Body Shop: The Engineering and Marketing of Life.* Washington, DC: Regnery, 1998.

Gina Kolata — *Clone: The Road to Dolly and the Path Ahead.* New York: William Morrow, 1998.

Marc Lappe and Britt Bailey — *Against the Grain: Biotechnology and the Corporate Takeover of Your Food.* Monroe, ME: Common Courage, 1998.

David Magnus and Alva Butcher, eds. — *Contemporary Genetic Technology: Scientific, Ethical, and Social Challenges.* Melbourne, FL: Krieger, 2000.

Henry I. Miller — *Policy Controversy in Biotechnology: An Insider's View.* Austin, TX: R.G. Landes, 1997.

Stephen Nottingham — *Eat Your Genes: How Genetically Modified Food Is Entering Our Diet.* New York: St. Martin's, 1998.

Martha Nussbaum and Cass Sunstein, eds. — *Clones and Clones: Facts and Fantasies About Human Cloning.* New York: W.W. Norton, 1997.

Gregory E. Pence, ed.	*Flesh of My Flesh: The Ethics of Cloning Humans.* New York: Rowman & Littlefield, 1998.
Michael Reiss and Roger Straughan	*Improving Nature: The Science and Ethics of Genetic Engineering.* New York: Cambridge University Press, 1996.
Jeremy Rifkin	*The Biotech Century: Harnessing the Gene and Remaking the World.* New York: Putnam, 1997.
Jane Rissler and Margaret Mellon	*The Ecological Risks of Engineered Crops.* Cambridge, MA: MIT Press, 1996.
Lee M. Silver	*Remaking Eden: Cloning and Beyond in a Brave New World.* New York: Avon, 1997.
Gregory B. Stock and John Campbell	*Engineering the Human Germline: An Exploration of the Science and Ethics of Altering the Genes We Pass to Our Children.* New York: Oxford University Press, 2000.
Laura Ticciati and Robin Ticciati	*Genetically Engineered Foods: Are They Safe? You Decide.* New York: Keats, 1998.

Index

regulator (CFTR), 22

DeGregori, Thomas R., 119
Denko, Showa, 112
Descartes, René, 33
DeSilva, Ashanti, 58
Diamond v. Chakrabarty, 176
disabilities. *See* persons with disabilities
discrimination. *See* genetic
   discrimination
diseases
   tracking genes to, 75
   see also gene therapy; genetic defects
Dixon, Bernard, 122
Dolly (sheep), 14, 91, 95
   and cloning success rate, 196
   and *Frankenstein*, 186, 187
   as natural and unnatural, 56
   public response to, 48, 100
   and stem cells, 149
drugs, genetically engineered, 42–43
DuPont, 115, 170

Edwards, Robert, 86–87
Ehlers, Vernon, 193
Eibert, Mark D., 191
embryos. *See* selective abortion
Enlightenment era, 32–33
Environmental Protection Agency
   (EPA), 123
eosinophilia myalgia syndrome (EMS),
   112
eugenics, 32
   vs. act of compassion, 81
   arguments against, 67–69
   defined, 15–16
   and genotype choice, 62
   government support of, 159
   history of, 47–48
   and human cloning, 195–96, 197
   negative vs. positive, 66–67
   and selective abortions, 88–89
   threat of, 32
Europe
   on genetically modified foods, 108,
      118, 121, 151
   as "green" culture, 152
European Patents Office, 166–67
European Union (EU), 108, 114
evolution
   and cloning restrictions, 97
   and genetically engineered humans,
      160
evolutionary psychology, 58–59
Exxon Valdez oil spill, 27

factory farming, 118
   see also genetically modified food

crops
farmers
   signing seed contracts, 143–44
   using ecological principles, 145–46
Federal Drug Administration (FDA),
   113
Feinstein, Dianne, 192
Feldbaum, Carl, 179
food
   animals genetically engineered for, 65
   biotechnology increasing production
      of, 136, 138
   need for increased production of,
      130–31, 134–35
   see also genetically modified food
crops
food allergies, 114, 127
Food and Drug Administration, 94–95
Foundation of Economic Trends, 170
France, 108, 120
Frankenstein (Shelley), 186–87
Friends of the Earth, 120
Funk, Walter, 47, 48
*Funk Brothers Seed Company v. Kalo
   Inoculant*, 174–75

Galapagos (Vonnegut), 97
Galton, Sir Francis, 15, 47
GATT Codex Alimentarius, 114
gene enhancement. *See* genetic
   enhancement
gene mapping. *See* Human Genome
   Project
gene protection technology, 144
General Agreement on Tariffs and
   Trade (GATT), 170
General Electric, 174
genes
   knowledge of, vs. changing, 59
   patenting, 167–68, 176–79
   as a work in progress, 59–60
   see also human genes
Genetech, 165
gene therapy, 14, 15, 20–22
   defined, 84
   first uses of, 21, 39–41
   vs. gene enhancement, 66–67, 73
   vs. genetically modified foods,
      122–23, 151–52
   is not controversial, 65–66
   need for further knowledge in, 43–44
   obstructing diseases through, 41–42
   opposition to, 69
   see also genetic engineering
genetically modified food crops, 15
   allergies from, 114
   antibiotic resistance from, 114–15
   campaign against, 118

214

114, 125–26
Lawrence Livermore Lab, 50
legislation. *See* genetic engineering, regulating
Lewontin, Richard, 104
lifespan, extending, 24
Locke, John, 33, 174
Losey, John, 123–24
L-tryptophan, 112
Luddites, 16, 156

Mack, Connie, 100
Maienschein, Jane, 150
medicine. *See* gene therapy
Merck, 169, 170
Michigan State University, 116–17, 164
milk
    medicines in, 22–23
    see also bovine growth hormone (rBGH)
Miller, Henry, 18, 127
monarch butterflies, 116, 123–24
Monsanto Corporation, 115, 117, 138, 142–43, 145, 164, 170
Moore, John, 168
Moore, Patrick, 127
Morton, Oliver, 55
mutations, 69, 95
Myriad Genetics, 170

National Biodiversity Institute, 169
National Bioethics Advisory Board (NBAC), 95
National Bioethics Advisory Commission on Cloning Human Beings, 102, 193–94
National Institute of Health, 149
Native Americans, 20
Nature (journal), 124
nature
    harnessing, 32–33
    power to change, 58–60
    products of, as patentable, 174–75, 176
Nazis, 15–16, 196
NewLeafRusset Burbank potato, 26
New Scientist (magazine), 123
Newton, Isaac, 33
Novartis, 115

oil spills, 27
Oliver, Melvin, 144
organic foods, 118, 131

parents
    of cloned children, 96
    cloning children for, 187–88

as genetically harming their children, 86
reproductive decisions by, 196–97
right to genetically modify children, 59
right to procreate, 194–95
patents, 46, 48–49
    debate on, 173–74, 178–79
    ethical aspects of, 163–64
    of human genes/body parts, 167–69
    and intellectual ownership, 179–81
    legal decisions on, 164–66
    opposition to, 170–71
    and plant breeding, 175–76
    on products of nature, 176–78
    purpose of, 174–75
    and seed contracts, 143–44
    third world vs. biotech companies on, 169–70
perfect-child syndrome, 79, 81–82
persons with disabilities
    achieving a good life, 85
    and genetic screening, 87–88
    and selective abortions, 79
    see also genetic defects
pesticides
    increase in, and genetically modified crops, 115
    and patents, 143–44
Peters, Ted, 74, 173, 177
Pfizer, 170
pharmaceutical companies, 48, 50–51
Pharmacia and Upjohn, 48
"pharming," 22–23
phenylketonuria (PKU), 60
plant breeding
    through nature, 132, 134
    and patents, 175–76
    see also genetically modified food crops
Plant Patent Act of 1930, 175
Plant Variety Protection Act of 1970, 175
population growth, 130
positive eugenics. *See* eugenics
Prakash, C.S., 133
prenatal genetic testing. *See* genetic screening
Pusztai, Arpad, 112, 114

Quigg, Donald J., 166
Quisenberry, Peter, 167

Raines, Lisa, 173
recombinant DNA technology, 14, 20
    drugs produced using, 42
    and gene mapping, 38
    regulating research on, 158–59